The

SAUSAGE DIRECTORY

A Guardian Book

Edited by Matthew Fort

GW00702918

FOURTH ESTATE · *London*

First published in Great Britain by

Fourth Estate Ltd
289 Westbourne Grove
London W11 2QA

A catalogue record for this book is available from the British
Library.

ISBN 1 85702 077 4

Designed by Jacky Wedgwood

Typeset by York House Typographic Ltd, London
Printed in Great Britain by Cox & Wyman Ltd, Reading

The

SAUSAGE DIRECTORY

*This book is respectfully dedicated
to all those amateurs of the sausage
who helped create it.*

Contents

Three Poems

●●●●●●●●●●●●●●●●●●●●●●●

A Love Which Dare Not Speak Its Name

Throbbing with gristle;
shaped like a Bishop's thumb;
a hoover-bag of meaty bits
without the bone.
You're not exactly handsome
yet you make woman moan
for in the frying pan of life
you stand (or lie) alone.

Spicy and rough
or smooth and secretive
to love you sausage
is to live.
What power you hold
beneath your tight brown skin.
Flavours unfold
after the fork's gone in.
Whether you're short and fat
or long and thin
something about you, sausage,
makes my senses swim.

I saw you first upon my nursery plate.
I covered you with ketchup
you were great.
I've had you with beans, in rolls
and pastry case
and when there was nothing else to have
you filled my face.

Spare me the jibes–
I've heard them all before.
Loving this porky snack's
within the law.
Loyal, hearty sausage
victim of smutty jokes
you're better than the measly chipolata
on most blokes.

LINDSAY MACRAE

A Poem for Colin Tyler's Sausages of Tetbury Traditional Meats

Miles cannot dim the image in the lover's eye,
Nor time to fade the hunger of the heart
I cannot let this worthy news slip by
The greatest taste on earth I must impart.
One mouthful will produce a heartfelt sigh
These sausages are supreme, so tender, full
'Tetbury Traditionals are the best,' I cry
So forward now I put my vote to all.
Merguez and Spicy Beef, Champagne or Cheese
And Tender sweet Toulouse for whom I'd die,
So many joys and all are made to please
Such is my love, I could not, would not lie.
Alas! my pen grows feeble, soon to still
My many loves, my friend, await me 'neath the grill.

JENNY WADE

Sausage and Mash

'If there's a dish
For which I wish
More frequent than the rest,
If there's a food
On which I brood
When starving or depressed,
If there's a thing that life can give
Which makes it worth our while to live
If there's an end
On which I'd spend
My last remaining cash,
It's a sausage, friend,
It's a sausage, friend,
It's a sausage, friend, and mash.

When Love is dead,
Ambition fled,
And pleasure, Lad, and Pash,
You'll still enjoy,
A sausage, boy,
A sausage, boy and mash.'

A P HERBERT

Lead Kindly Light

Sausages are The Great British Passion. They are the universal food. From Lands End to John O'Groats, everybody has their favourite. Their diversity is legion. Great sausages are to be found the length and breadth of Britain. So, sadly, can a great deal of not-so-great sausages.

The Sausage Directory has been painstakingly assembled through the efforts of sausage lovers to help others find a decent sausage within easy reach, wherever they may be.

The Joy of the Sausage

I will not be didactic about this. I am a breakfast sausage man. I rarely eat sausages at any other time of day, although I am partial to the odd sausage sandwich (preferably between two slices of soft, white bread of the utmost purity. Only bread made by the dreaded Chorleywood process is soft enough to mould itself around the slices of sausage and make an easy-to-eat mouthful. But that is by the by).

Nevertheless, should I ever run a restaurant it would serve only sausages. They would come hot. They would come cold. Some would be grilled over wood. Others would simmer quietly in water. And most would sizzle seductively in frying pans.

They would be served by cheery, breezy, efficient waiters and waitresses that knew the difference between service and servility. And they would come in the company of mash or cabbage or beans or apple or chips or whatever else would be the special of the day. And they would come from the four corners of the globe.

The sausage is the universal food. There are more varieties of sausage than there are human languages (Anthony and Araminta Hippersley-Cox list over five hundred in their masterly and monumental *Book of the Sausage*).

There are sausages of pork, of beef, beef and pork, of chickens' and pigs' blood, of porpoises' blood, veal, venison, chitterlings, wild boar and horse. There are sausages of duck, and sausages of chicken, sausages of mutton and sausages of tripe. In the charming *Unmentionable Cuisine* (University Press of Virginia), Calvin W. Schwabe lists a sausage made from pig's uterus, popular among ancient Romans; the Kiszka z krwia of Poland, made with the snout and the feet of a pig; a sausage made from a lamb's liver and coconut cream – Kalegi – from India, and the Hungarian Töltött libanyak made from stuffing the neck of a goose.

Nibble, I can hear myself coaxing the wary customer, a Reinsdyrpølse of Norway, made of reindeer meat. Sink your teeth into a link of Sin Ap Yeung Cheung of China, or sniff the luxuriant odour of the Saucisses Soudjouk of the Levant. If these don't appeal, perhaps the Hildersheimer Streichleberwursts or the Debrecener Rohwurst might be to your taste. No? Well how about a Makkara? A Lukanka, the spicy pork sausage of Bulgaria? Merguez of Algeria? Or Umbria's celebrated Mazzafegati? What about a Greek Soudzoukakia? I would woo the vegetarian with a Glamorgan sausage made from Caerphilly, breadcrumbs and mustard. I should lure the fish fanatic with a Cervelas Maigre à la Benedictine, of which the principal ingredients are eel and carp, and perhaps whip up the odd concoction of my own – an oyster sausage or one made from guinea pigs.

I have eaten sausages in a good many places, and I have put away some notable specimens in my time. There was one memorable platter of exquisite little chaps, moist and sparklingly spiced, in Erice in Sicily. They came on the plate plain and unadorned, for they needed no adornment. When in my dotage, I sit in my room in the Blue Bayou Sunset Hostel, a rug tucked around my knees, staring quietly into the past, I will recall with a shiver of delight the warm, succulent, musky vapour that rose up out of the andouillette into which I had plunged my knife in the station buffet at Clermond-Ferrand so many years before. But when it comes to the crunch, my heart is reserved for the English sausage. Here, the sausage is almost the last, nationally available craft food. There are artists of the pigs' cheek and shoulder, spice and breadcrumb, casing and herb up and down the land. The evidence of their skill is to be found in the plump, sinuous attractions of the Cumberland, coiled like a somnolent python, or the no-nonsense, big-as-a-boxer's-fist, six-to-a-pound bunches favoured in the Midlands. Chipolatas are included under certain circumstances, and we must admit hog's pudding and haggis into the Pantheon of supreme sausages. The Lincolnshire sausage has its supporters, and one can occasionally come across the pork, veal and beef suet Oxford sausage.

But in the final analysis each fine sausage should be known after its maker. Whatever grand, regional tradition the craftperson finds him or herself working in, the end product will bear the imprint of their personality; their taste. There are plenty of butchers who have been making the same sausages to the same basic recipe for generations. There are others who have pioneered new breeds of sausage.

One of the notable developments in the sausage sector is the way in which butchers have responded to the demand for sausage exotica. It is now quite possible to find good merguez, Toulouse, boerewors, and cotecchino all made on the premises, as it were. There has been the rise of the specialist sausage shop, such as Cowman's of Clitheroe in Lancashire, Simply Sausages and Biggles in London, O'Hagans of Greenwich and Lindy's in Caterham. These pyrotechnicians of the sausage will think nothing of conjuring up forty or fifty varieties – designer sausages of chicken and banana, steak and kidney sausages, Scarborough Fair sausages involving parsley, sage, rosemary and thyme, and sausages of pork and pink champagne. But these, I think, are sausages for the special occasion; the occasional sausage. Indeed, for some of the combinations put about, I can think of no occasion that I would be tempted to eat them, but then I am a fusty traditionalist. They are not the everyday sausage of comfort and familiarity.

•••

The Romans may have been responsible for bringing the sausage to Britain. Sir Mortimer Wheeler suggested that there might even have been a sausage factory at St Albans, using horsemeat.

Richard II was partial to a sausage made from chicken and pigs: 'Take hens and pork and boil them together. Take the flesh and hew it small and grind it all to dust. Take grated bread and mix it well with broth, and add it to the yolks of eggs. Boil it, and put therein powder of ginger, sugar, saffron and salt – and look that it be stiff.'

•••

The Great Quest

The *Guardian* Great Sausage Quest started out as an act of charity.

A couple of years ago I was hit by a personal tragedy. Vic Franklin, butcher of High Street, Twyford, Berks, and sausage-maker supreme, closed for the last time. It was an old story. The property in a burgeoning London commuter dormitory town was worth more as a site to develop than it was as the centre for one of the country's great craft skills. On top of that, the grandson of the founder was fed up with working a twelve hour day, seven days a week; fed up with trying to find and keep skilled staff and fed up with not having a holiday. He had my sympathies, but it left me with a yawning chasm in my life. I and my family had been putting back Mr Franklin's finest pork bangers every Sunday breakfast, and sometimes in between, for over thirty years. I am not proclaiming these sausages as the finest ever made by the hand of Man, although I would hold them to be so. I suspect that when you have grown up with a sausage, then that is the sausage against which all subsequent sausages will be judged.

Even if they weren't everybody's ultimate sausage, Vic Franklin's had most of the right qualities: they were moist; they were succulent; they had a pleasing density when cooked. The meat had been ground to the right coarseness, and spiced and peppered to a nicety, and they had a well rounded, square shouldered kind of flavour. Excuse me while I wipe away a tear. As my brother Tom wrote in his obituary for the shop in the *Financial Times*, 'It would take a top notch lyric poet – a Herrick or Herbert of the kitchen range – to do justice to these sausages.' I bought a final five pounds on the day that they closed, and eaked them out over succeeding Sundays until they were gone.

And then what? Was Sunday to be turned into a sausage free zone? Too ghastly to contemplate.

I wrote an article explaining my plight in the *Weekend Guardian*. I appealed to the decency and generosity of *Guardian* readers. If anyone could recommend a decent sausage, I said, I would procure it, taste it and, when I had tasted all, would declare one The People's Sausage, and so solve my problem and live off it on Sunday for the rest of my life. I underestimated just how decent and generous *Guardian* readers would be. Very nearly five hundred people wrote in. Some were businesslike and brisk, giving names and addresses only; some put forward their champion with a pleasing simplicity, and some wrote panegyrics that the poet laureate would have been proud to lend his name to.

But the whole venture had clearly got wildly out of control. I mean, I was faced with the possibility of munching my way through over three hundred sausages, by the time I had weeded out the duplicates. Do you know what three hundred sausages look like? I do now and, let me tell you, it's a daunting sight. Clearly I needed help. I went back to the readers. If they could recommend, perhaps they could help taste as well. With the help of our own splendid Marketing Department and the dauntless and charmingly named Sausage Bureau, a specialist arm of the Meat and Livestock Commission, we organised a grand tasting at the Butcher's Hall in London. Butchers were asked to send a pound of the pick of their sausages there. In the event the butchers took pity on us. One hundred and fifty actually sent in their sausages and, believe you me, that was quite enough.

We cooked them and three panels – each consisting of three Guardian readers and a chairperson–nibbled, nuzzled, chewed and swallowed their way through fifty sausages per panel. Each panel recommended two sausages which went through to the final. We were then strengthened by celebrity judges Robert Elms, Helen Lederer, Rowley Leigh, chef of Kensington Palace, and Gary Rhodes of The Greenhouse. Flavour was marked out of ten; texture likewise; appearance rated five. We reckoned that most sausages only look enticing when you're in the mood. It's how they acquit themselves in the gob that really matters. And so they came, two by two, anonymous to us, on numbered plates to preserve all ethical niceties. Fifty sausages may not seem a lot to you, dear sausage lover, but let me assure you it represents a mountain of protein, fat, gristle, herbs, spices and other substances that you probably wouldn't like to think about.

One of the most impressive features about the whole thing was the variety of sausages giving of their best. A banger, you might think, is just a banger. Oh, no it isn't! There are pork bangers, and beef bangers, and pork and beef bangers, and cheese and pork, and pork and lamb, and pork with this herb and that spice. Curiously enough, three of the sausages that went through to the final had a whiff of garlic about them, hardly the traditional combo, you'd have thought, but proving unbeatable in the heat of the competition.

So the final of the first ever *Guardian* Great Sausage Quest was a celebration of the vitality and variety of British sausages, and a bit of an eye opener. Here are the results:

THE 1991 PEOPLE'S SAUSAGE

The Country Sausage with garlic from Merrivale Foods of Falmouth, Cornwall.

RUNNERS-UP

Old Charley's from L.J. Smith of East Leigh, Hants.

Pork Sausage from Riverford Farms, Totnes, Devon.

There was one inescapable conclusion to all of this. There were a lot of people out there whose passion for the sausage was quite as great as my own. It seemed only right that we should have another Quest, only we would try and broaden it out, encourage regional specialists, nibble and savour sausages that, for whatever reason, did not get to the tasting tray last year.

So the 1992 Quest was launched on March 14. This year we made use of the good offices of Bass Taverns, both to gather nominations and to hold regional heats. We did not want The Quest to become just another Metropolitan romp. The essence of the sausage is its regionality, reflecting the different meat and herb or spicing combinations in favour locally. For example, the

Scots are keen on a pure beef banger, while the Welsh are partial to a pork and beef or lamb and pork mix, and south country folk go for pure pork. The response has been an enthusiastic as it was last year, which goes to show that the passion for sausages cannot wither.

We have held tastings in Birmingham, Bristol, London and Warrington, which represent a pretty fair regional distribution. At each of these a total of thirty-one good men and women and true – *Guardian* readers and Bass drinkers all – have done the selecting. The sausage with the highest marks was declared the regional champion, and the top six sausages from each of the regional heats went through to the final taste-off, again at the Butchers' Hall in London.

I have gone into the process in some detail because I want to emphasise why this is the People's Sausage Quest. Believe it or not, there are plenty of sausage competitions which are judged by professionals for professionals. Yes, there are even professional sausage tasters. But there had never before been a competition which was judged by the people for the people – i.e. those of us who actually fork out our £1 and whatever pence for a pound of plump, gleaming bunches of six or eight. And, as I have seen, there has been some disparity between the sausages that the experts have picked as the *ne plus ultra* of the day, and those selected by our various panels. I should add that the experts did not mind in the least. These men are true lovers of the sausage, and can appreciate others' passions as well.

Anyway, from this serious selection process, in which we tasted legions and legions of sausages, we have chosen sixty worthy sausage-makers from all over England to be listed as 'The Judges' Selections' in *The Sausage Directory*.

JUDGES' COMMENTS

'This is a pub sausage which you pay £1 for and reckon 50p would be generous.'

'I don't suppose that we're allowed to spit them out?'

'It tastes better once you've stopped eating it, if you know what I mean.'

'I'm sausaged out.'

'Ooh, I just love the knobby end.'

'I'm a *Telegraph* man, myself, and I can't stand garlic.'

●●●

Last year we ate 300,000 tonnes of sausages or twelve pounds each. That's enough to make a rope of sausages to the moon and halfway back.

●●●

Champion Qualities

There are as many serious sausages as there are serious sausage-makers.

When we began the first Quest, there were long and serious discussions about what we were looking for. In any professional sausage competition, the number of individual links – as single sausages are known in the trade – are specified. They are weighed and inspected uncooked. They are weighed and inspected cooked. They are judged on appearance, texture and flavour in that order.

That was all a bit complicated for us. We wanted to come up with a sausage that anyone could buy by going into the particular shop and ordering a pound or so. We wanted to judge our sausages by the way in which anyone judges sausages at their own table. Flavour comes first in my book, followed closely by texture. A sausage has got to feel right between the teeth, have the right density or crumbliness, depending on your preference. And appearance comes last. Any sausage that has been properly cooked should look terrific – brown, glistening with promise, perhaps a slight curl of steam rising up from its plump flank. Eat me, it whispers.

But too often it turns to sawdust and old must when you dig your gnashers in.

When it comes to deciding what makes a decent banger, I suspect that it depends on how you were brought up. Anyone whose palate was moulded by the fiery spices of merguez of Morocco or the chorizo of Spain may find the sweet mildness of the south country banger a bit mild for their taste. Those for whom the sage brought an aromatic note to the ground pork for the infant nostril may cavil at the coarse rankness of the beef sausage the Scots and northerners prefer.

Personally I don't really like herbs in my sausage. I am a pork man, and pepper and perhaps a sprinkling of mace is what I look for. Nevertheless, tasting sausages from all over the country has been a salutary experience. So many of them, it seemed to us, were terrible: stale, dried herbs with that dusty, musty flavour, or herbs which had been added with a casual disregard for the flavour of anything else. Some oozed fat like an Exxon Valdez oil slick, others were sad and sour. Still others crumbled at the touch because bread or rusk provided a higher component than perhaps it should have done. But each of them had a champion. Each had been recommended personally by someone, frequently with glowing encomiums that would have had the most imaginative advertising copywriter blushing with shame. This is why I have included a list of readers' recommendations at the back of this book.

Technically speaking, a sausage has to fulfill certain criteria by law. A pork sausage must have a total meat content of 65%, and at least half that meat – i.e. a piffling 32.5% of the whole beast – must be lean meat. In other words, 50% could be fat, skin, rind, gristle or sinew known as connective tissue. Worse, it could even be MRM – mechanically recovered meat, something akin to slurry. Filler (rusk) can take up another 10%, but 20% by volume because rusk swells with fat and water, and up to 10% can be devoted to extras such as salt, herbs, spices, soya and milk proteins and additives.

Just to cheer you up some more, meat is usually about 75% water. More is added at the chopping stage in the form of iced water to keep the ingredients cool. Naturally, a good deal is absorbed by the meat.

Whenever I pick up a packet of pre-packed sausages of which the ingredients have been printed, I look to see how much meat there actually is in each plump link. 'Min 65% meat' a good many proclaim. I look at the two inch wonder, and think that if one and a half inches are meat (and what kind of meat at that) then what does the other half inch consist of? Gunge of various kinds, evidently. And that only goes for pork sausage. If you are addicted to the non-pork chaps, then you only get 50% meat, i.e. half your sausage is probably not what you think it is.

There are also those little extras. There's salt, which helps bring out the flavour and makes the meat protein stick together; phosphates to improve water retention; herbs and spices for flavour; soya protein and milk to improve the texture; colours to improve the appearance; antioxidants to stop the fat going rancid; sulphur dioxide to prolong shelf life; stabilisers; dextrose to sweeten the flavour, prevent oxidation and help browning; sodium caseinate to maintain the colour and looks, sodium ascorbate to help preserve the looks; monosodium glutamate to enhance the flavour.

Recently we have seen the arrival of that abomination, the Low Fat Sausage. Our concern with how much fat we eat is truly reaching ridiculous proportions. Everything we eat has to be lean and mean. We tamper around with the genetic make-up of animals to reduce the fat that they naturally produce, so that we can go on eating the amounts of meat we are accustomed to, and we still worry about it. If you're really concerned, the answer is quite simple: eat less meat; eat better, i.e. better raised meat; don't eat less fatty meat – fat is essential for flavour and less fat means less flavour. Anyway sausage lovers should abhor the Low Fat Sausage on more practical grounds. An analysis of six popular brands of low fat sausages by *Which?* (November 1990) revealed that they weren't significantly lower in fat or higher in lean meat than many of the premium sausages, and weren't liked by the tasting panel either for appearance or taste. So there!

So, when people leap to the defence of the English banger against the monstrous tyranny of Brussels, I don't leap with them. It is true that we should be allowed to eat rubbish if we want to, but I can't help thinking that we wouldn't once we had eaten a more classy act.

And so the *Guardian* Sausage Quest proves.

• •

In seventeenth century Poland, a good cook in a nobleman's house had to know a dozen ways of making kielbabas, the great Polish sausage. But an aristocratic cook had to have twenty-four at his disposal.

The Romans were prodigious sausage-makers. The word sausage derives from the Latin salsicium, meaning something that has been salted, and there was a sausage known as *farcima* from which has become farce or forcemeat these days.

• •

Ten Tips for Tastier Sausages

●●●

1. Check the meat content. As a rule, any sausage with less than 75% meat will be a rotten sausage.

2. Check that at least 50% of that is lean meat.

3. Check that your sausage is made with natural casings, i.e. lambs' or pigs' intestines.

4. Ask how frequently they are made.

5. Check that they are made on the premises, or come from a dependable, regular supplier.

6. A freshly made sausage should have a soft, plump, gleam to it. Don't buy anything that looks sad or dull or tired.

7. Don't buy anything that is too wet, either. That will mean they have only just been made and will split when cooked.

8. Complain vigorously if they don't come up to scratch.

9. Don't give all the offending batch to the dog. Take them back, and ask if the butcher would eat them.

10. Don't buy a mass produced sausage if you can possibly help it.

●●●

According to the Oxford English Dictionary the first specific reference in English came in a fifteenth century vocabulary: 'Salsicia, a sawsage.'

By 1755 Samuel Johnson brought the sausage back to earth in his Dictionary: 'Sausage, a roll or ball made commonly of pork or veal, and sometimes beef, minced very small, with salt and spice; sometimes it is stuffed into the guts of fowls, and sometimes rolled only in flour.' Interestingly, he makes no reference to casings.

●●●

Cooking the Sausage

I am a great believer in the frying pan. I'll go further. I am a great believer in the heavy cast iron frying pan blackened with heat and with age, gleaming genially with layers of accumulated grease that have fused into a natural non-stick surface.

Respectfully lay those gleaming, pristine sausages across the centre of the pan and, leave them there, gently cooking, for a very long time (long enough to make a pot of tea, take it upstairs to your slumbering partner, rouse him or her, share a few agreeable moments of domestic repose, play 'This is the way the lady rides' with the favourite infant of the moment, wash, dress, and slope downstairs again) about forty or fifty minutes in all. That's the ideal.

There are those that will have it otherwise, but in my experience frying sausages is by far the superior way of cooking them even if you cannot go for the council of perfection and go for the full forty minutes. It is only through frying, and slow frying at that, that you allow the meat to gradually heat through, encouraging the polite exchange of flavours among the various parts and the fat to leach out through the semi-permeable skin. At the end of the process, you should have a moist, sweet flavoured mouthful, the contents of which have consolidated their position to a seductive nicety, yielding gently to the teeth.

It seems to me that the fiercer and the more direct the heat, the worse it is for the sausage. It is difficult for the sausage to flourish, to show off its best when subjected to the naked flame of the grill. It dries out the surface; it bullies the meat; it smothers the herbs and spices; it encourages unsightly bursting and it is hardly preferable to roasting them or baking them in the oven.

The ovenproof sausage has yet to be made. Sausages emerge from the oven dried and wrinkled as octogenarians in the Florida sun. They appear as flaccid as an over-ripe banana but, on closer acquaintance, prove as unyielding as old leather. Baking sausages seems to have the effect of thickening their skins and giving them the texture of old vellum. Convenient though it may be, particularly if you're cooking in bulk, baking is no way to treat a decent sausage.

However, even baking them is better than cooking them over the barbecue. The barbecue, is, of course, the apotheosis of naked flame cookery. It is no coincidence that the Afrikaans word for barbecue is braaivleis, meaning burnt meat, or, as I like to interpret it more poetically, burnt flesh. Place a sausage over all but the most gentle of glowing coals, and it will burst asunder and quickly form an impenetrable carbonated carapace which will protect the inside from all but the most desperate of teeth and which, on finally breaking through, will release a burst of searing steam into the mouth and reveal an inside which still, miraculously, is quite raw.

One way round this problem is, I am reliably informed, an old New Zealand trick. You blanch the sausages for ten minutes in boiling water some time before the barbecue. Within reason it doesn't matter how long before. Now, in this semi-cooked state, they are ready for the fiery furnace. In a trice they acquire their black armour casing, but at least they are cooked within. Naturally, they will have no flavour apart from the agreeable taste of charcoal, but no matter. With half a dozen of these inside them your guests will not get seven seas over on Pimms or Sangria. And they will be happy with far smaller helpings of chops or chicken or steaks, or the more expensive cuts that you have so thoughtfully provided.

Under no circumstances whatsoever prick an English sausage. It does not require, or deserve, such treatment. If you do, you will only allow a good deal of the natural juices to flow out during cooking, making the inside drier and lessening the flavour. The argument that you need to prick in order to prevent bursting is tosh. It's true that meat, and air – there could be air pockets in your sausage mixture – swell while you're cooking the blighters but, if you're dealing with a quality sausage of the kind that you find in this book, and you treat them with the care and reverence they deserve – i.e. don't try and cook them too quickly – then they will not burst. Or should not burst. The skins will gradually expand to accommodate the macho meat, and the fats will ooze out.

If you're really worried about the burst sausage phenomenon, and you are prepared to sacrifice a deal of aesthetic and gastronomic perfection then bake away. The even distribution of heat prevents this. The only sausages for pricking are sausages for boiling, for example the Italian cotecchino or the French saucisson-cervelas de Lyons, boudins, black puddings and the haggis.

The sausage and the microwave is a relationship of which I have no experience, not having a microwave. However, the editors of the admirable Reader's Digest *Microwave Cookbook* clearly believe that it can be done because they include a recipe for Cumberland Sausage with Glazed Onions.

There is one final consideration for the kitchen. In an ideal world we will pop along to the sausage-maker supreme of our choice whenever we feel like a sample of his or her art, and purchase a link or two. Alas, life does not always run along such agreeable lines. There may have to be days, weeks or even months between visits, so you may have to stock up with enough to keep you going in between. Sausages, of course, do have quite a long fridge life – up to a week can be safely recommended, naturally as long as you keep them well away from cooked meats.

But then sausages also freeze admirably. They should be frozen on wire racks and then popped inside bags, but you can freeze them in bags right away. Just make sure to mark on the outside what they are and how many; and eat them within six months. When you do get round to eating them, take them out well in advance. How good any frozen food will taste depends to a large extent on the thawing, and sausages need to be unwrapped and thawed slowly if they are to give of their best.

••

The early Church strongly disapproved of the sausage.

••

Ten Tips for Caring Cooks

1. Give a slight twist to the link before severing it from its fellow.

2. Make sure that you sever them cleanly – no tearing of the skin.

3. Do not prick your sausage.

4. Fry for as long as possible over a very low heat – 40 minutes is an ideal length.

5. Try to ensure even distribution of heat.

6. Turn the sausages after 20 minutes.

7. Grilling is quicker than frying, but is not so good for the sausages. Grill for 12–15 minutes, turning frequently.

8. Bake if you must at Gas Mark 4 for 20 minutes or so, depending on the thickness of the sausages.

9. Blanch sausages for 10 minutes in boiling water if you want to barbecue them.

10. The burnt caramel that forms at the base of the pan during cooking is reserved for the cook.

Sausages are celebratory food. It has been suggested that the phallic shape and spicy ingredients made them a popular nibble at the saucy Lupercalian and Floralian festivals. Young Swabians eat sausages at Pfingstenfruhstuck (egg-and-sausage breakfast) outside on Whitsun. The Italians devour Zampone con lenticchie (pig's trotter sausage with lentils) on New Year's Eve and New Year's Day.

Straight pork sausages account for 51% of all sales; beef and pork for 40%; straight beef for 7%; and 'others' for 2%. Beef sausages are most popular in Scotland. In Wales the preference is for beef and pork.

Let them not go naked
····················
onto the plate
···················

Let me confess it right away: I am a ketchup man, Heinz Tomato Ketchup at that. To many this is heresy, but for me there is something about the sweetness and piquancy of the sauce that helps bring out and balance the meatiness, preferred pepperiness and burnt skin of the sausage. And that splash of scarlet on the pristine plate looks so handsome alongside the gleaming armour of the rank of sausages.

There are those who swear by HP or Daddies or a whole palette of other sauces. Their pedigree is as good as the tomato ketchup, and their function the same. They replace the sweet acidity of the tomato with fruitier flavours, and frequently with zippier spices. It's a matter of choice; of what you're used to.

There is a good deal to be said for good, simple gravy, particularly if you are serving them with mashed potato. Naturally I am not referring to the disgusting and ersatz gunk that comes out of pots and packets. I mean the stuff that you make yourself out of beef or veal or chicken stock, enlivened, if you want, with a dash of red or white wine, or even sherry, or perhaps cider, if you want a sweet touch, and then thickened with a thimble of cornflour which is carefully cooked out, i.e. thoroughly incorporated. The thickening is important – it shouldn't be too thick, mind, but that slightly heavier texture, similar to the ketchups, seems to suit the sausage. Regional purists may go for particular variations. Onion gravy for example, is particularly suited to toad-in-the-hole.

Of course, mustard is the preferred condiment of many, and these days there are almost as many varieties of mustard as there are of sausage. If you want to go the mustard route, the fruitier grain mustards, particularly those of English origin seem to me to be more agreeable. They lack the happy ceremony of lifting the teaspoonful of fine yellow powder out of the tin with the rounded corners and yellow label, and mixing it with milk and water, or milk and sherry as we used to do when I was a lad, but, on the other hand, their fruitier, browner flavours seem to suit the sausage better, and the seeds add an agreeable crunchy texture to the mouthful.

On the other hand, English mustard of traditional fieriness comes into its own with the cold sausage, a different thing, and a delicacy in its own right. Given the range of mustards now being churned out by every urban refugee to the countryside, it would be invidious to recommend just one. In many cases, different sausages need different mustards. That's why, in my view, the mustards of Dijon are better with the sausages of France. An English mustard sits uneasily on the andouillette, and a salsiccie from Modena nestles up to the Mostarda di Cremona easily and naturally.

Had Mostarda di Cremona originated in this country, it would have been called the Tracklement of Shrewsbury or some such. I am not sure from what forgotten tome the Olde English word 'tracklement' was resurrected, but it smacks to me more of smart rural marketing than of decent culinary invention. Not that the products called 'tracklements' aren't any good. Some of them are. But 'tracklement'? I mean, well really!

When it comes to vegetables, we are talking recipes, and recipes aplenty you will find on the following pages. As a general observation, chips are currently the most wanted – if not the most gastronomically elevated – veg when it comes to British sausage fanciers. I prefer mash myself. And cabbage, in red or choucroute form. Apples and onions are also a good match. Beans, be they baked and out of a tin or braised and homemade, have a traditional ring to them. And recently we have seen the emergence of polenta, the Italian equivalent to mash made from maize flour, but this may only be a temporary gastro-fad.

But a good sausage is proof against any such hoydenish modern tendencies. That's one of its many virtues. It will hold its own in any company. It can be lifted from daily domesticity to the heights of gastronomic appreciation by the company it keeps, and its own intrinsic qualities.

'Besides these cares, the Captain had to keep his eye on a diminutive frying-pan, in which some sausages were hissing and bubbling in the most musical manner. . . "My lady lass," said the Captain, "cheer up and try to eat a deal. Stand by, my deary! Liver wing it is. Sarse it is. Sassage it is. And potato." '

Charles Dickens – *Dombey and Son*

Recipes
••••••••••••••

If you have a good sausage, you can grill or fry it and be
eating well in mere minutes. But you can also cook it
with other ingredients to make a more elaborate dish.
Here are some fairly basic ways, culled from European
and American cuisines as well as British, of doing just
that. The classic partners for sausages include potatoes,
cabbage, pulses and beans. All of these feature prominently here.

Some sausage recipes call for a particular type. Spanish recipes will characteristically specify *chorizos*,
Polish recipes a *kielbasa* or smoked sausage, and French
recipes one of the wide variety used in that sausage-
loving country. The aim in this section is to give recipes
that are not sausage-specific. If you can get Polish
smoked sausage to use in Bigos (page 40), that's great.
If you cannot, the product from your local sausagery will
do just as well.

In general, these recipes assume that your sausages
are fairly well seasoned. If they're on the mild side,
increase the quantity of seasoning as appropriate. You
won't go wrong by using your judgement where this
overrides the recipe.

Sausages and Mussels

Sausages and shellfish may seem an unlikely combination, but they're used together in French, Spanish,
and Cajun cooking among others. If you can't get
mussels, try squid or prawns.

1 bag of mussels (usually 1 kg, 2.2 lbs)
1 small handful fresh coriander
1–2 tbsps extra-virgin olive oil
1 clove garlic
60ml (4 tbsps) dry white wine
1 small onion
500g (1 lb) well flavoured sausages

Clean mussels in cold water, discarding any that are
open. Mince garlic and heat the oil over a low heat in a

large saucepan or stockpot. Cook garlic for a minute or so, then add the mussels and wine and cook, covered, for 4–5 minutes or so. Stir at least twice to make sure the mussels are well distributed in the pot. As soon as they're done, turn the heat off and leave uncovered.

While the mussels are cooking, cut the sausages in discs and chop the onion. Heat more oil in a frying pan and cook the onions and sausage quickly. As soon as they're done, add them to the mussel pot and stir well; you can heat them up for a minute more if the mussels have cooled. Serve immediately with plenty of bread to mop up the juices.

Sausages and Beans

Sausages and beans are another classic combination. Here's a version from the USA, based on New England-style Pork and Beans.

500g (1 lb) dried red or white beans
1 large onion (around 200g, 6 oz)
2 small carrots
3 fat cloves of garlic
4 slices of ginger
125g (4 oz) smoked pork knuckle or smoked bacon
1 tbsp dried mixed spices such as *herbes de Provence*
50g (2 oz) brown sugar (enough to fill a measuring cup to the 100ml mark)
150ml (5 fl oz) maple syrup or Golden Syrup
30ml (2 tbsps) Worcester Sauce

Soak the beans overnight or boil for 30 minutes and leave for an hour. Chop the onion, carrot, garlic and ginger, and cut the bacon (if using) into 2″ lengths. Combine all ingredients except the sausage into a large casserole and bring to the boil, then cook gently either on the stove or in a slow oven (around 150°C, 300°F, Gas 2) for 3 hours or more. (There is a great deal of latitude when cooking this dish.) Half an hour before you want to eat, put the whole sausage (or sausage pieces) in the casserole and let them cook with the beans.

Cassoulet

Cassoulet is the French answer to Pork and Beans, but much more complex and sophisticated. The real thing takes hours to prepare and cook. This version is far simpler and easier, if inauthentic. It will feed 8–10 people easily.

500g (1 lb) dried white beans
2 large carrots
4 cloves of garlic
1 large onion
4 tbsps vegetable oil or (preferably) bacon or goose or
    duck fat
1 bouquet garni or 3–4 tbsps fresh herbs
a handful of parsley
a large piece of pork rind or a piece of belly of pork
chicken or beef stock as needed (at least 450ml, 16 fl
    oz)

Meats (*per person*):
1 large, well flavoured sausage
1 lamb chop, preferably from the shoulder
1 small pork spare rib chop

Soak the beans overnight or boil for 30 minutes and leave for an hour. Drain well. Roughly chop the carrot and garlic, and stick the cloves into the peeled onion. Heat 2 tbsps of the oil or fat in a large casserole and gently cook the carrots and garlic for a few minutes, then put in the beans, onion, herbs and pork, adding just enough stock to moisten them. Cook over a very gentle heat for 1 hour or so, till the beans are soft but still retain their structure.

Meanwhile, heat the remaining fat in a frying pan and brown the meats on all sides. When the beans have finished their hour of cooking, forcibly stick the browned meats into the centre of the casserole. Add more stock if needed and cook for another hour or more, peeking every 15 minutes to check on the stock. (Add more as needed.) Serve piping hot.

Sausage Rolls

This is a basic recipe for one of the favourite sausage preparations. To vary it, add grated cheese, dried mustard, fresh herbs, or a little chopped onion to the sausage meat.

500g (1 lb) puff pastry
500g (1 lb) sausages, or sausage meat
1 egg, beaten

If using whole sausages, remove the skins. Roll out the pastry in a large rectangle around ¼″ thick. Roll the sausage meat into a cylinder around ½″ in diameter. Cut a piece of sausage the same length as the long side of the pastry rectangle. Place the cylinder along one side of the pastry, around 2″ in from the edge. Add any extra flavourings you care for, then brush the edge with egg and fold it over the sausage. Press firmly, making sure the sausage is in contact with the pastry at every point. Cut this roll away from the pastry and then into smaller lengths, anything from 1½″ to 4″. Refrigerate while you continue the process until the pastry and sausage are used up.

To cook the rolls: Preheat the oven to 200°C (400°F, Gas 6). Make a slash or two in each roll to provide a steam vent, and brush the tops with egg. Place the rolls on an ungreased baking sheet and bake at the top of the oven for 20–30 minutes, till the sausage is cooked and the pastry brown and puffed up. Remove to a wire rack and eat either hot, warm or room temperature.

Sausages with Hot Potato Salad

This classic of French bistro cooking is usually made with a boiling sausage such as *saucisse de Toulouse*. But it is just as good with a well flavoured banger.

500g (1 lb) waxy potatoes
2 slices of onion
a small handful of parsley
5 tbsps (75ml) extra-virgin olive oil
2 tbsps wine vinegar
60ml (4 tbsps) dry white wine
500g (1 lb) sausages

Boil the potatoes gently in their skins for 30–40 minutes. While they're cooking, mince the onion and parsley and combine with the oil, vinegar, and wine. Season well, salt and pepper. When the potatoes seem to be around 10 minutes from being done, grill or fry the sausages. The aim is to have them finished just as the potatoes are ready. When the potatoes are cooked, peel them if you wish (it isn't necessary) and toss with the dressing while still hot. Serve immediately with pickles and mustard, and accompany with a glass of Alsace Sylvaner or Riesling.

Toad-in-the-Hole

At its simplest, this eminently comforting dish is nothing more than sausages and pancake batter. Try adding extra zing by seasoning the batter with curry powder, dried mixed herbs, or a bit of powdered mustard. Use the lesser weight of flour for a lighter batter, the higher for a denser version.

For the batter:
300ml (½ pint) milk
125–150g (4–5 oz) plain white flour, or a combination
   of white and whole wheat
a size 1 egg
a large pinch of salt

For the sausages:
1–2 tbsps vegetable oil
500g (1 lb) sausages

Preheat the oven to 200°C (400°F, Gas 6). Make the batter by sieving together the dry ingredients (including all extra flavourings), then adding the beaten egg and the milk gradually. Whisk all the ingredients together, but do not beat them too long; allow to rest for 30 minutes. Any lumps remaining will work out during the resting time.

   Heat the oil in a frying pan (preferably non-stick) and quickly brown the sausages over a fairly brisk heat. The aim at this point is to do nothing more than brown them, so don't worry if they're still quite pink inside. Put them in a large ovenproof dish and pour on the batter. Bake at the middle level of the oven for 30–35 minutes, till the batter is cooked through and the top nicely browned.

The Ultimate Sausage Sandwich

Well, maybe the penultimate. But exceptionally tasty whatever its ranking. These quantities are per sandwich.

a few slices of onion
2 good sausages
1 tbsp good tomato ketchup
1 tbsp Worcester sauce
a drop of chili sauce
½–1 tsp English or Dijon mustard
1 good roll, or length of baguette, around the length
    of the 2 sausages
2 slices of ripe, red tomato

Fry the onion slowly, in a tiny bit of butter, till it's very soft. Remove to a small bowl and keep warm by the side of the hob (or put in the microwave for a final reheating). Get the sausages cooking in the onion pan, or under the grill. While they're cooking, whisk together the ketchup, Worcester sauce, chili sauce and mustard. Cut the roll in half and remove most of the soft crumb from the interior. Lay on the mixed sauces and the tomato slices; you can halve the slices if necessary. When the sausages are done, reheat the onion if necessary. Put the sausages in the bread, lay on the onion, and press together the two halves of the roll to close up the sandwich. This is a real mess to eat, which is part of its charm.

Smothered Sausages

Smothering is a technique beloved of Cajun cooking, and this recipe is Cajun in conception.

1 large onion
3–4 red and green peppers
6 stalks of celery
2 fat cloves of garlic
500g (1 lb) sausages

a large pinch of dried thyme or a large sprig of fresh
  thyme
110ml (4 fl oz) dry white wine or chicken stock
2 spring onions or a small handful of parsley

Preheat the oven to 180°C (350°F, Gas 4). Cut the
vegetables into slices around ¼″ thick and put the
sausages in a casserole or baking dish which is large
enough to hold them in one layer. Add the vegetables
and the herbs, trying to ensure that the sausages are
fully covered. Pour on the wine or stock, cover the pot,
and cook at the centre of the oven for 45–90 minutes, till
the vegetables are nice and soft and the sausages fully
cooked.

If you wish, you can reduce the cooking liquid by
rapid boiling and then degreasing it. You could also
thicken it by mixing 2 tbsps of flour with a little of the
cooking liquid and then stirring it in. The spring onions
or parsley should be chopped, if you're using them, and
added to the dish just before serving.

Sausages with Lentils

It's important to use lentils that have their hulls intact.
Choose brown, green, or especially 'lentilles de Puy',
the aristocrats of the lentil kingdom. The flavourings in
this dish were suggested by *Guardian* reader Alyson
Dunn, of Linthorpe, Middlesborough, Cleveland.

500g (1 lb) sausages
500g (1 lb) lentils
1 orange
2 red onions
6 spring onions
2 thick slices of fresh ginger
2 large cloves of garlic
4 large tomatoes
2 tbsps extra-virgin olive oil
300–400ml vegetable stock, chicken stock, or water
2 tbsps chopped parsley

If you want to, cut the sausages into 1–2″ lengths;
otherwise just leave them whole. Peel the zest from the
orange and cut into fine shreds; squeeze out the juice
and reserve. Slice the red and spring onions thin and

mince the ginger and garlic. Coarsely chop the tomatoes. Heat the oil in a saucepan and slowly cook the vegetables for a few minutes, just to soften and release some of their juices. Add the lentils and 300ml of the stock or water, and bring to the boil. Simmer gently for 15 minutes.

Now add the sausages or sausage pieces, making sure they're well buried in the lentils. Cook for another 25–30 minutes, topping up with extra stock or water if necessary, till the lentils are done. (Don't worry if it takes longer than this: the sausages can easily tolerate extra cooking.)

Sausage and Sweet Potato Casserole

This takes its inspiration from a dish described by M.F.K. Fisher in *How to Cook a Wolf* (1942). The effect of the potatoes and seasonings is a fairly sweet one, so using a well herbed or even a spicy sausage will provide just the right balance of flavours.

750g (1½ lbs) sweet potatoes
500g (1 lb) sausages
¼ tsp each of powdered cinnamon, nutmeg, and
   cloves
60ml (4 tbsps) milk
2 tbsps honey or maple sugar

Cook the potatoes thoroughly (in boiling water or the microwave) and let them sit until they're cool enough to handle easily. Preheat the oven to 230°C (450°F, Gas 8). Mash the potatoes roughly with the spices, milk and honey/maple syrup. Put the sausages on top and bake in the oven till the sausages are brown and sizzling.

Sausages with Stir-Fried Cabbage

Sausages and cabbage are another classic combination. Braising the cabbage is perhaps the standard treatment, and a very good one. Stir-frying the cabbage and then adding the sausages for the final stage of cooking, as in this recipe, also works well.

½ head of Savoy cabbage (around 1½–2 lbs)
3–4 tbsps extra-virgin olive oil

1 clove of garlic
1 tsp caraway or fennel seeds
a few leaves/sprigs of fresh herbs – thyme, rosemary,
  sage
500g (1 lb) sausages
100ml (4 fl oz) stock or water or dry white wine

Cut out the core of the cabbage and shred it using a
large, sharp knife or the slicing disc on a food processor.
Heat the oil in a large frying pan or casserole (the
cabbage is very bulky when raw). When it is very hot,
put in the cabbage and stir-fry briskly for 2–3 minutes.
The cabbage should blacken in spots, which is entirely
acceptable. Mince the garlic and add to the pan along
with the caraway/fennel seeds, and stir thoroughly. Now
turn down the heat and let the cabbage cook for 5–10
minutes, stirring occasionally.

Roughly tear or chop the herbs. When it is heated all
the way through but still very crunchy, put in the
sausages, herbs, and stock (or water or wine). Cover the
pan and cook for another 20–30 minutes, turning the
sausages once.

Sausages in Sherry

This is based on Nicholas Butcher's recipe (in *The
Spanish Kitchen*, Papermac) for 'Salchichas al Jerez'.
Butcher points out that while Spanish-style salchichas
are best, any good chipolata will serve the purpose. If
you don't have sherry, use a robust table wine either red
or white.

1 tbsp (approx.) extra-virgin olive oil, vegetable oil, or
  lard
500g (1 lb) sausages
3–4 cloves of garlic, sliced or minced
1 tsp paprika
around 90ml (3 fl oz) *fino* sherry

Heat enough oil to film the bottom of a frying pan,
preferably non-stick. When the oil is hot, cook the
sausages rapidly until lightly browned all over. Turn
down the heat to low and add the garlic and paprika.
When the heat has died right down, pour in the sherry;
there should be enough to come around ¼ of the way

up the sausages. Cover the pan and cook gently for 15–25 minutes, till the sausages are just cooked, and serve with bread or potatoes. A little flat-leaf parsley makes a nice garnish.

Michel Roux's Christmas Stuffing

This recipe was given to *Guardian* columnist Richard Ehrlich by Michel Roux, chef of the Waterside Inn and co-author (with his brother Albert) of such books as *French Country Cooking*. Chef Roux's recipe uses pork fillet and pork fat in proportions of 2:1, but it works almost as well with pork sausage. These quantities are enough for the neck cavity of a 14lb bird. *Note*: Like all sensible cooks, M. Roux advises against stuffing the main cavity because this increases the cooking time to the point at which overcooking is inevitable.

20g (¾ oz) butter
50g (2 oz) onion, fine chopped
100g (4 oz) mushrooms, minced
50g (2 oz) cubed white bread
100ml (scant 4 fl oz) milk
600g (around 1¼ lbs) pork sausages
20g (¾ oz) parsley, minced
10g (around ½ tbsp) salt
2g (around $\frac{1}{6}$ tsp) black pepper
100ml (scant 4 fl oz) single cream
20ml (1¼ tbsps) cognac
1 egg

Divide the butter between two frying pans and gently cook the onions and mushrooms separately till translucent or soft. Soak the bread in the milk until well softened, then lightly squeeze out the bread and discard the milk. Refrigerate all ingredients till needed.

Combine everything except the cream, cognac and egg. Mix well. Stirring steadily with a wooden spoon, slowly add the cream, cognac and finally the egg. The mixture is now ready for cooking, but you should test for seasoning by poaching a spoonful and tasting it.

Stuff the neck cavity and roll any surplus into a sausage shape to cook, wrapped in aluminium foil, alongside the bird.

Bigos

Bigos, 'hunter's stew', is the Polish national dish. Closely related to *choucroute garnie*, it is another instance of the affinity between sausage and cabbage. Bigos is traditionally made with a smoked sausage but the ordinary variety can be substituted if you add smoked bacon to the mixture. This recipe is modelled after one in *The Polish Kitchen* by Mary Pininska (Papermac). *Note*: It should be started 24 hours in advance.

2 medium onions
50g (2 oz) butter
1 kilo (2 lbs approx.) sauerkraut
2 400g (14 oz) cans of Italian plum tomatoes
1 small fresh cabbage
300ml (around 12–13 fl oz) beef stock
125 g (4 oz) smoked bacon
2 tbsps honey
500g (1 lb) sausages

The day before you want to eat this, chop the onions, melt the butter in a large casserole, and gently cook the onions till they're lightly browned. In the meantime, chop the bacon in 2″ pieces, rinse the sauerkraut, and shred the fresh cabbage. Add to the casserole with the tomatoes and stock. Bring to the boil, cover, then cook over a low heat or in a slow oven (around 170°C, 325°F, Gas 3) for 1 hour. The next day, cut the sausages in half and cook in the casserole for another hour or so. If you like, the dish can be left for another day and reheated before serving.

Cabbage Stuffed with Sausages

Stuffed cabbage is a great winter dish, and this variant is easier than many versions. Use homemade tomato sauce if possible.

1 head of Savoy cabbage
8 sausages (around 500g, 1 lb)
1 tsp paprika
60ml (4 tbsps) sour cream
around 225ml (8 fl oz) tomato sauce

Preheat oven to 180°C (350°F, Gas 4). Remove 8 of the

large outside leaves from the cabbage and blanch until soft in plenty of salted water. Drain well and cut away the thick part of the central rib from each leaf. Pat them dry. Place one sausage on each leaf, with the sausage at right angles to the rib. Top each with a sprinkling of paprika, a dribble of sour cream, and a healthy dose of salt and pepper. Roll them up and pack into a gratin or baking dish which will hold them tightly in a single layer; the dish may be buttered first if you wish.

Pour on the tomato sauce, adding more if there doesn't seem to be enough to douse the cabbage thoroughly. Cover with aluminium foil and bake in the centre of the oven for an hour or so, till the sauce is bubbling and the sausages thoroughly cooked. You could, in the meantime, use the remaining cabbage to make a coleslaw or a stir-fry with garlic and caraway seeds.

Sausages and Tomatoes

This is based on a recipe in Rena Salaman's *Greek Food*. The original calls for green peppers and Italian or Greek sweet sausages. If using plain bangers do not omit the extra spices.

1 large onion (optional)
500g (1 lb) sausages
1 generous tsp dried oregano (optional)
1 generous tsp fennel seeds (optional)
1 generous tsp coriander seeds (optional)
1 400g (14 oz) can of Italian plum tomatoes

Preheat oven to 200°C (400°F, Gas 6). If using the onion, slice it thin and scatter over the bottom of a gratin or baking dish. Heat a non-stick pan over a moderate heat and brown the sausages lightly. Drain off excess fat and put in the baking dish with the seasonings, followed last of all by the tomatoes. Season well with salt and pepper, cover loosely with aluminium foil, and bake for 25–35 minutes at the centre of the oven.

Baked Sausage, Onion, and Potatoes

There are few dishes simpler than this one, and few more satisfying on a cold winter's night.

500g (1 lb) sausages
500g (1 lb) onions
500g (1 lb) baking potatoes
1 large sprig of fresh rosemary, or 1 tbsp dried
2 tbsps extra-virgin olive oil

Preheat the oven to 200°C (400°F, Gas 6). Cut the sausages, onions and potatoes into pieces approximately 1″ square and coarsely chop the rosemary (if using fresh). Put the oil in a roasting tray and coat the potatoes in it. Cook at the top of the oven for 10 minutes, then add the onions. Cook for another 10 minutes and add the sausages and herbs plus a generous grinding of black pepper. Toss well and cook for another 30–35 minutes, and serve with a salad and a bottle of robust red wine.

Sausages in White Wine

This is a simplified version of a recipe in Escoffier's *Ma Cuisine*. Use well herbed sausages.

500g (1 lb) sausages
1 tbsp white flour
225ml (8 fl oz) strong beef stock
100ml (3½ fl oz) dry white wine
2 tbsps chopped mixed fresh herbs: thyme, tarragon, parsley, sage

Cook the sausages in a large frying pan, adding a little butter if you wish. When they're just done, remove to a serving platter and keep warm. Turn the heat down and pour out excess cooking fat, then sprinkle the flour in the pan and let it cook for a few seconds with the remaining fat. When it's dissolved, pour in the stock and blend well. Turn the heat up, add the wine, and boil rapidly to reduce by one half. Stir in the herbs, cook for a few seconds more, and pour sauce over the sausages. Serve with mashed potatoes and a salad.

Chicken Breasts Stuffed with Sausage

This is based on a recipe in *American Charcuterie* by Victoria Wise. If you can't get chipolatas, use sausage meat formed into little torpedo shapes. These quantities serve four.

4 chipolata-size sausages
2 chicken breasts, bone removed
6 cloves of garlic
450ml (16 fl oz) white or red wine
1 tbsp fresh tarragon, or 1 tsp dried

Cook the sausages in a little butter or poach them till barely done. Halve the chicken breasts lengthwise and flatten them slightly with a kitchen mallet or the flat of a cleaver. Now wrap a sausage in each half and secure it with toothpicks.

Heat the frying pan over a medium heat and melt a little more butter. Put in the chicken and season with salt and pepper. Brown on all sides for 6–7 minutes. Add the garlic and cook for another minute, then add the wine and tarragon. Turn heat down to low and cook for another 5–10 minutes, till the chicken is just done. Remove to a hot platter, turn the heat up to high, and boil the cooking liquid till it's reduced by around 75%. Pour over the chicken and serve with saffron rice.

Sausages with Chestnuts and Apples

Chestnuts and apples are two of the great partners for a sausage. This simple recipe combines all three of them.

500g (1 lb) sausages
500g (1 lb) chestnuts
500g (1 lb) eating apples
110ml (4 fl oz) beef or chicken stock
1 tbsp Cognac (optional)

Cover the chestnuts in water and bring to the boil, then simmer for 20 minutes or so. Peel them and poach till barely soft in clean water or, better still, some meat stock. Turn off heat and set aside till needed. Fry the sausages in a little butter till barely cooked. Remove and set aside.

Peel and core the apples, and cut in pieces around the same size as the chestnuts. Heat a little more butter in the frying pan and gently cook the apples for 5-10 minutes, till they're soft but still have quite a lot of crunch left in them. Add the chestnuts and sausages and pour in the stock and Cognac (if using). Cook for a couple of minutes more, just to heat everything through, and serve with potatoes or good bread.

••

The Spanish of the fifteenth century used to include chorizo, a pork sausage, in stews for hanging from the rafters to show that they weren't either Jews or Muslim.

27% of sausage lovers eat them for breakfast and 57% at their evening meal. 16% presumably graze on them all through the day.

••

Bangers 'n' Plonk

There is only one descriptive factor common to sausages: each is a stuffed tube enclosed in an edible membrane. Thereafter, various design changes come into it. To begin with, contents will vary from one sausage to another; the lengths will differ; and the cooking methods will be dissimilar. Likely as not, there are more types of sausage than there are human languages.

For the purposes of a rumination upon the wines to drink with the blessed things, then, I feel it necessary to closely identify the sort of sausage I am talking about before I suggest which wines might be best drunk with it. Take chorizo. This ripe masterpiece of Iberian cuisine can be fat, long and round, sliced and eaten cold; or it can be small and slim, and either grilled or roasted or used as a crucial ingredient in a stew. There is no doubt in my mind that the best wine for this sausage in all its forms and in all its various guises is one which is wood-aged and made from the tempranillo grape. Riojas are the most famous examples of this sort of wine but my favourite tempranillo wine with chorizo whether it be cold as a tapas, grilled in thin slices and placed atop a salad, or just plain oven roasted is a tempranillo from the Raimat wine company of the Costers del Segre region of northern Spain. This exhibits more of a soft chocolate spiciness than the vanilla undertones of Rioja and works even better. With merguez sausages, those spicy vipers from north Africa, I would go for Chilean cabernet sauvignon or merlot from the Cousino Macul winery, one or other of the new Bulgarian Country Red wines made from a blend of cabernet sauvignon and cinsaut grape varieties (both Sainsbury and Tesco have excellent examples of these), or an Australian shiraz (and just about the cheapest example of this is Safeway's which even comes in a three litre wine box with reusable tap – perfect for sausage parties or for sausage eaters who only enjoy the odd glass of wine and so dislike opening a whole bottle). With barbecued sausages of any kind, the shiraz grape variety seems heaven sent. The burnt, smoky flavour imparted to a sausage by this method of cooking needs a spicy, smooth, soothing wine with a broad personality and there is hardly an Australian shiraz which won't fit this particular bill. What's more, the bill can be extremely low. With Australia climbing a mountain of debt yet sinking under a lake of wine, winemakers are desperate to sell their wines at whatever prices they can get. Bargains abound.

With more conventional ways of cooking sausages, frying, grilling or roasting, and with more conventional sorts of sausage, I enjoy Côtes du Rhone red wines. One of the best names to look out for here is E. Guigal. Should you see those words on a bottle of red Côtes du Rhone you have a perfect marriage on your hands and it matters not a whit whether the sausage be of the spicy, herby Cumberland persuasion, or a truncheon sized monster stuffed with garlic. Monsieur Guigal turns out exemplary sausage wines. With British-style sausages, many French wines are excellent. From the Loire, Chinon and Bourgeuil are perfect. And from the south-west, the wines of Cahors, Fronton, and Corbières (especially the 1989 Chateau Cabriac – this Corbières goes for under six quid the magnum at Asda supermarkets and though the fruit seems austere coming as it does after the glorious woody bouquet, the wine quickly turns to nectar in the mouth with grilled pork sausages, fried onions, and mashed potatoes). Italy also makes many great wines to accompany sausages.

Barolo and Barbera are good with fried sausages, and so too is Chianti. These wines have a superb sunny fruitiness which is worth paying extra for if the sausages are equally out of the common rut. However, a word of warning here: do not invest in an exquisite Barbera, for example, if you propose first dunking your sausage in one of those pungent mustards made with wine vinegar and swarming with seeds. Any subtlety and complexity the wine posseses will be wiped out by such a potent condiment, whatever considerable merits it may otherwise demonstrate. A faint smear of English mustard, although initially hotter, is a more sympathetic companion in these circumstances though this must be applied with a demur knife otherwise the money you have invested in the wine will be wasted. If you must have dollops of mustard with your sausage, then the only wine in the world with the muscle not to be completely overwhelmed by the embrace is a first-class zinfandel from California. This zingy, zesty grape variety is America's own and, well-vinified, has the warmth and richness to be considered the supreme sausage wine.

••

The Elizabethans liked a white pudding which contained raisins, dates, cloves, mace, sugar, saffron, pigs' liver, eggs and breadcrumbs.

••

Bangers 'n' Beer

It was the toughest assignment of my career. 'Write about beer to drink with sausages,' ordered Fort, the Carnivore King.

'I don't eat meat,' I mumbled. 'Copy by the twentieth,' he grated, adjusting his green eye-shade to a menacing angle.

Fearing I could end up as beer correspondent of the *Sunday Sport*, I dug deep into my memory banks to think what a sausage tasted like and then rang Bill O'Hagan, purveyor of bangers to beer festivals.

'A meatless sausage, please,' I said. 'Impossible,' he replied. 'I have perfected a marvellous filling but I just cannot get a skin that will satisfy the Vegetarian Society.

'But you can get skinless sausages,' I pointed out. 'They are not *real* sausages,' he thundered. He will market his filling as vegeburgers, but that was no help to me.

Well, I make a mean soya sausage, liberally laced with herbs and spices, and that will have to suffice as a template. And what we need are rich, herby, spicy and aromatic beers that will bring out the best in a banger, flesh-free or not.

If your tipple is lager then you will have to ignore the poor apologies made in Britain. They are too thin and flabby to do justice to the dish. Above all, they lack the rich hop character that is essential to complement full flavoured food.

Pilsner Urquell, the original Pils beer from Czechoslovakia, is the ideal lager. They eat a lot of sausage in that country and Urquell, with its massive Saatz hop character and full bodied malt and vanilla aroma and palate, could have been designed for the job in hand.

From the United States, Brooklyn Lager is brewed to a pre-Prohibition recipe. It's an all-malt brew and has a superb hop aroma and flavour. It has thirty units of bitterness, more than double the insipid mainstream American beers, and the brewer uses home-grown Cascade hops and German Hallertau. The scintillating hoppiness of the beer, which is available in selected branches of Sainsbury's, will marry well with sausages that are spicy and laced with tangy mustard.

An American ale with a booming hop note comes from the Anchor Brewery in San Francisco. Liberty Ale is less well known than the flagship Anchor Steam Beer, but I adore its enormous Cascade hop appeal. It is available in Fuller's off-licences.

Fullers, the West London independent, brew some splendidly hoppy beers themselves. They are best known for their London Pride and Extra Special Bitter, but my favourite of the range is the modest 3.5 per cent alcohol Chiswick Bitter. It has a lightly fruity, quenching aroma and palate, and plenty of hop character from the generous use of Challenger, Goldings, Northdown and Target varieties.

Fuller's friendly London rivals, Youngs of Wandsworth, have appreciably improved the character of their strong Special Bitter. A touch too malty for me in the past, the beer is now 'dry hopped' with peppery Goldings – this means that every cask of the beer gets a generous handful of hops.

The result is a revelation, a beer with a zing of hops that underscores the rich malt and fruit of aroma and palate.

Bass have gone in the opposite direction with Draught Bass, the most widely available cask beer in Britain. No doubt to please the accountants, the beer no longer gets a dose of hops in the cask but its nutting maltiness will go well with sausages that are not too overpowering in taste.

I would choose in preference from the Bass stable the original India Pale Ale, Worthington White Shield, a bottle-conditioned beer with vast hop and fruit character.

Among other national brands, the tart and citric Tetley Bitter and the robust and fruity Ind Coope Burton Ale, both from Allied Breweries, go well with robust food flavours.

Dark beers should not be ignored. Guinness stout seems to accompany most known dishes, from oysters to fish and chips. Its deep bitterness from roasted barley and a good hop rate would point up a banger, especially if it gets slightly overdone on the 'barbie'.

Choose your Guinness with care, though. Avoid the

flashy 'draught in a can' and go for the world classic, the bottle-conditioned Guinness Original, available only in pubs.

Stout's historic stable-mate, porter, is back in fashion. Youngs of London have just launched a porter and Whitbread have one on test-market in 250 of their pubs.

Eldridge Pope of Dorchester have a new Blackdown Porter with a fine hoppy, coffee character. The renowned Yorkshire brewers, Timothy Taylor of Keighley, brew an occasional creamy porter. If that is not available then go for their stunningly fruity and hoppy Landlord best bitter.

In the Midlands, Ruddles, mercifully free now from the Grand Met embrace, have in Ruddles County a rounded fruity ale with Goldings hop character, fine with a ploughman's lunch of ripe cheese and pickles, so it should be beneficial with a banger.

Belgium offers a wonderfully tangy beer in the shape of Hoegaarden White, just launched here by the Stella Artois group. A top-fermenting beer using wheat as well as barley malt, the hops are supplemented by coriander and curaçao. It is enticingly fruity, bitter-sweet and spicy and would go well with food or as a palate-cleanser after a meal.

And now, with the Pilsner Urquell chilling in the fridge, I must add a dash of paprika to the soya sausage mix. . . .

●●

'The euil eaten sausedge came gushing out after', is the picturesque description from D. Rowland in Lazarillo (1586).

In 1573 J. Baret describes 'A pudding called a sawsage'.

The Confession of J. Browne, Jesuit (1641), raises the spectre of religion in the history of the sausage: 'He brought them of his Holinesses' bread, and wine, and other rarities, as Bolognean sassages, and such dainties.'

●●

The 1992 Sausage Quest
Final

After six fiercely contested heats around the country, 00 sausages reached the grand final, held at the Butchers' Hall in London. Gathered round the table, forks at the ready, were: chefs Marco Pierre White and Gary Rhodes; Minister for Food Nicholas Soames; artist Jeff Rawle; comedians Vic Reeves and Bob Mortimer; DJ Alan Freeman; volunteer *Guardian* readers C. Lamb, Mike Brown, Katrina Amos, Neil Young and Jane Charteris; poet Lindsay Macrae; presenter of TV's 'The Word' Katie Puckrick; and of course myself.

Some judges were free with their opinions, others held close counsel. All chewed, slurped, chomped, ruminated and, on occasion, spat with furrowed brows as the hopeful finalists arrived sizzling from the kitchens. Only one sausage could claim the august title of 'The 1992 People's Sausage', and only one butcher could adorn his shop with the magnificently plump and stately carved wood trophy. But five more would have the consolation of being runners-up.

Here are some of their general comments:

'I like to eat meat every day, especially in its piped form.'
Bob Mortimer

'The British people will benefit from your decisions.'
Myself, putting heart into the judges.

'I'm big on sausages. My ideal is firm and spicy. I'm talking about things you put in your mouth.'
Katie Puckrick

'Sausages are the stuff of life. They are an important part of the British public's diet. . . . Well, they're certainly an important part of mine.'
Nicholas Soames

'The width is more important than the length.'
Marco Pierre White

And here, arranged – after the six finalists – in alphabetical order of city/county, are the results of all our deliberations. . .

THE 1992 PEOPLE'S SAUSAGE

Country Fayre Pork & Chives

John Walton Butchers

Like a Grand National Winner, this sausage was a stayer, showing great consistency throughout the competition. It had an excellent tight, firm texture. It was juicy without being fatty. The herbs supported, not disguised, the meat. And as it sat there on the plate, you just wanted to eat it.

COMMENTS FROM THE FINAL FRY-IN:

'Big bangers are best. Very meaty. Great flavour. Texture right. Simply the best.' (*Mike Brown*)

'Juicy. Well rounded flavour.' (*C. Lamb*)

'Moist and good fat content.' (*Gary Rhodes*)

'Very good. Good herby flavour. Similar to 325 but better texture.' (*Lindsay Macrae*)

'Smelt better than it tasted.' (*Nicholas Soames*)

'Interesting appearance. You can see real herbs. Consistent texture.' (*Jeff Rawle*)

'Meaty.' (*Katie Puckrik*)

'Perfumed.' (*Katrina Amos*)

For address and further comments see page 97.

Pork & Leek

Alan Bennett Ltd

I followed this sausage from the regional tasting in Birmingham through to the final. I kept recognising it like an old friend. Not, perhaps, a sausage to set the world alight, but sober, safe, and sensible – and easy to eat. Although, needless to say, not all the jury agreed with me.

COMMENTS:

'Looks good and tastes good. Lacking substance.' (*Neil Young*)

'Bog standard sausage. Tasted better than it looked as does the pig from whence it came.' (*Bob Mortimer*)

'Rubbery and bland. Not enough meat or flavour.' (*Lindsay Macrae*)

'A little salty. The taste didn't linger.' (*Alan Freeman*)

'Soft. Fruity.' (*C. Lamb*)

'Onion flavour. Soft texture. Rather good.' (*Jeff Rawle*)

'Texture too fine.' (*Gary Rhodes*)

'Too mild.' (*Katie Puckrik*)

'Good texture.' (*Nicholas Soames*)

'Aesthetically pleasing, flecked with herbs although you can't taste them.' (*Lindsay Macrae*)

See page 108.

Italian Sausage

Felix van den Berghe

I thought that this was a splendid sausage, and was rather surprised when others did not agree with me. There was a touch of sweetness about the meat. The texture was firm and succulent and juicy. But the Italian touch – fennel mostly – proved too much for the orthodox palate.

COMMENTS:

'Greetings sausage pickers. This is the sausage to spend your life with. Almost perfection.' (*Alan Freeman*)

'Yuk!' (*Anon*)

'Nasty aniseed flavour.' (*Mike Brown*)

'Clearly a foreign sausage. Has been injected with winegums.' (*Bob Mortimer*)

'Very good smell. Delicious sausage.' (*Nicholas Soames*)

'Totally chewy. Liquorice taste. Would never buy or eat.' (*Gary Rhodes*)

'Good balance.' (*Katrina Amos*)

'Good meaty sausage.' (*Lindsay Macrae*)

See page 61.

RUNNER-UP

Garlic Pork

Collins Butchers/Knowle Farm Smoked Food

Garlic and pork seem to go together, like Vic & Bob or Marks & Spencer. That whiff of the exotic brings out the sweetness of the meat. Not dissimilar to last year's winner. Quite dry, but firm. Looks good too.

COMMENTS:

'Very good sausage. Right balance of herbs and meat. Very fine texture. Plain looking.' (*Alan Freeman*)

'Splendid sausage. Almost exotic flavour. Delicious.' (*Nicholas Soames*)

'Dry and meaty.' (*C. Lamb*)

'Spicy, herby, good consistent texture.' (*Jeff Rawle*)

'Spicy.' (*Katie Puckrik*)

'Initial high impact eventually leading to disappointment and a sense of having been cheated perhaps by a shepherd.' (*Bob Mortimer*)

'Chewy texture. Too herby in flavour.' (*Gary Rhodes*)

See page 103.

Traditional Pork

Fieldsahead

A short, fat, friendly fellow. Nice to look at. A sausage you'd like to take home with you. And eat. And you'd find it as chunky within as on the outside, with a high meat content to judge by dense texture and the full flavour.

COMMENTS:

'A little chewy. Full flavour.' (*Katrina Amos*)

'Great looks. Small, fat, juicy. Good, meaty flavour.' (*Mike Brown*)

'Greasy aftertaste. Good rough texture. Lovely look.' (*Jane Charteris*)

'Short and dumpy. Inconsistent colour. Tight texture. Meaty. Gentle full flavour. Well rounded.' (*C. Lamb*)

'A little lumpy and greasy.' (*Jeff Rawle*)

'Texture slightly grainy and dry. Good seasoning.' (*Gary Rhodes*)

'Mild. Slightly crumbly.' (*Katie Puckrik*)

'A low impact sausage. Could be quite frightening if eaten wearing a cat suit.' (*Bob Mortimer*)

See page 63.

Traditional Pork & Sage

Gibson & Coe

This one rather split the jury, but the ayes had it. Basically, if you like a fine chopped sausage of fairly dense texture and pronounced herby flavour, this is the one for you. The quality isn't in doubt (unless you hate the kind of sausage this sausage is).

COMMENTS:

'A splendid looking sausage. Perhaps a little spicy.' (*Alan Freeman*)

'Best sausage.' (*Lindsay Macrae*)

'Very ordinary smell.' (*Nicholas Soames*)

'Good seasoning. Slightly too fine a texture.' (*Gary Rhodes*)

'Punchy.' (*Katrina Amos*)

'A nice looker but watery. Nice accompaniment to some beer.' (*Bob Mortimer*)

'Not very "British" in flavour. Well messed about with in spice additions.' (*Mike Brown*)

'Relatively dry. Liquorice aftertaste.' (*Neil Young*)

'Delicious.' (*Jane Charteris*)

See page 105.

The Judges' Selections

Beef

Strathmore Larder
Cowford
Menmuir
Brechin
Angus DD9 6SF

Tel: 0356 660 238

Meat content: 75%

Great beefy flavour, but finely minced. Texture quite dense, but mouthfilling, lipsmacking, and oh, yes, I'll-have-that-off-your-plate-if-you're-not-quick-about-it flavour.

COMMENTS:

'A classy sausage. Fine and firm.'

'A bit rubbery for my taste. Flavour OK.'

'Not too salty. Sort of dark meat flavour.'

'A bit Oxo-y.'

'Give my sausage back.'

OTHER SAUSAGES:

Smoked pork, smoked beef, pork, lamb & mint, venison, pork & venison.

Lamb with Provençale Herbs

Keith Macey
Rose Cottage
Lower Road
Cookham Rise
Berks SL6 9EH

Tel: 0628 521128/0628 784685

Meat content: 80%

One of the few lamb sausages, and this lamb did not die in vain. Lively and personable without being passionate. Fine texture.

COMMENTS:

'First one to have a distinctive smell. Nicely spiced/herbed.'

'Pleasantly spiced.'

'Good.'

OTHER SAUSAGES:

Prime Somerset pork, Olde English, spicy garlic pork, pork with fresh tomatoes, pork with leek, pork with apple, Lincoln pork with sage, very hot & spicy, special chicken & herbs, lamb with sweet garden mint, special beef, turkey & pork.

Sausages made to order. Minimum order: 10lbs

Italian

Felix van den Berghe
40 High Street
Westbury-on-Trym
Bristol BS9 3DZ

Tel: 0272 509484

Meat content: 100%

Done the Italians proud. Excellent sausage. Coarse cut, close texture. Punchy flavour and nicely spread. Not unlike Italian football.

COMMENTS:

'Robust flavour and good texture.'

'Overall a very exciting sausage.'

'Not too exotic. Quite delicate. Rather nice.'

'A good sausage.'

OTHER SAUSAGES:

Felix van der Berghe make over thirty different sausages, including pork & coriander (also highly rated), Lincolnshire, chicken & garlic, chicken Louisiana, chicken tandoori, beef & horseradish, beef madras, pork celery & stilton, lamb apple & calvados.

Tasty Pork

Josef Packert, Continental Butcher
19 Nelson Street
Bristol BS1 2DA

Tel: 0272 268294

Meat content: 70%

Nice but not naughty. A personable sausage. Short on
character, but a sound companion at breakfast or supper, hot or cold. Finely ground.

COMMENTS:

'Good, ordinary sausage. A bit too finely cut for my
taste.'

'A good standard sausage. Nothing exotic, but I
enjoyed it.'

'Tasty.'

OTHER SAUSAGES:

Cumberland, pork & garlic, pork & tomato, curried
pork, old English, farmhouse, bratwurst.

Traditional Pork

Fieldsahead
3 Greenways
Sawtry
Cambridgeshire

Tel: 0487 830595

Meat content: 67%

Hunky and chunky and stylish, too. Sweet, with a hint of gaminess at the back of the teeth. Herbs kept well under control. Moist and firm. Seconds, please.

COMMENTS:

'An emperor among vassals.'

'Coarse. Very spicy.'

'Rather too coarse in texture. Flavour very encouraging.'

'Plenty of pork.'

'Scout camp.'

'Very tasty. Nice porky flavour.'

'Gummy flavour. Stale spice.'

OTHER SAUSAGES:

Pork & garlic, vegetarian.

Yorkshire Pork

Mr Lazonby's
Unit 7
Station Road
Stokesley
Nr Middlesborough
Cleveland
(Available through Presto, Safeway and Co-ops.)

Tel: 0642 712540

Meat content: 85%

Dare I say this has the hallmarks of the Southern style –
sweet pork, quite finely cut, dense-like texture. And
very acceptable, too.

COMMENTS:

'This would be a winner.'

'Very pleasant. Could take it anywhere.'

'This sausage may be less tasty than it seemed.'

'Smells good but doesn't follow through.'

'Gentle flavour.'

OTHER SAUSAGES:

Thin pork, thick pork, chipolata, Cumberland, special
Cumberland, tomato, thin pork & beef, thick pork &
beef, tikka, tandoori, barbecue, Yorkshire, Guisbor-
ough (pork & peppers), Roseberry (pork & cheese &
pepper), Stokesley (pork, curry & garlic), Mexican,
Butcher's Choice, American.

Cumberland

Richard Woodall
Lane End
Waberthwaite
Nr Millom
Cumbria

Tel: 0229 717237

Meat content: 98%

Classic Cumberland. A pleasure to see coiled on the plate. A fine meaty, peppery mouthful or two or three. All right – meal in its own right.

COMMENTS:

'Very good. Meaty, well minced, balanced seasoning. An excellent ordinary sausage.'

'What I think of as a sausage.'

'Lovely flavour – not too salty. Meaty. Unpretentious.'

'Warming food.'

OTHER SAUSAGES:

Thin breakfast.

Plain Pork

Farrows
Pond Street
Chesterfield
Derbyshire S40 2LE

Tel: 0246 272734

Meat content: 65%

More Carmen Miranda than Plain Jane. A spicy not-so-little number, and moist and meaty. Good, firm texture.

COMMENTS:

'Starts well, but is rather too spicy.'

'A little too moist, and spice takes over as you eat it.'

'Not overspiced.'

OTHER SAUSAGES:

Pork & tomato.

Pork with Organic Leeks

Scott Hallam's Riber Farm Shop
Greenways Farm
Riber Village
Matlock
Derbyshire DE4 5JU

Tel: 0629 583108

Meat content: 73%

Evidently the leek is to the British banger what garlic is to the European. Here, organic or not, touching its forelock to good pork.

COMMENTS:

'Very good taste. Appearance rather lumpy.'

'A bit too salty. Otherwise an attractive flavour.'

'The leek does not really add to the sum total.'

'Leek is pleasantly moderate. Not too intrusive.'

OTHER SAUSAGES:

Cumberland, pork & garlic, pork & chives, pork & herb, Auntie Mary's plain pork, pork & chestnut, pork & mushroom, pork & apple, pork & tomato, pork & leek, pork & celery, Chinese pork, pork & peppers, pork & curry, pork & chilli, Cajun, Hawaiian pork, pork countryside, pork tropical, cheesy pork, venison, game, bacon & liver & roast onion, seafood, beef & mustard & dill, lamb & mint, Yorkshire beef, pork countryside, Lincolnshire, Derbyshire (lamb & beef), ham & tomato, bratwurst, gluten free, pork & nut.

Garlic Pork

Food Naturally Ltd
1 Eddlestons Farm
Copplestone
Crediton
Devon EX17 5LE

Tel: 0363 83794

Meat content: 80%

Fine all-rounder. Easy on the eye. Nicely chewy. Well flavoured. Whisp of garlic, setting off sweetness of pork.

COMMENTS:

'Interesting. Fairly subtle. Sufficiently chewy. One would like to eat more again.'

'Good all-round taste and texture.'

'Tasty.'

'Looks like a boomerang.'

OTHER SAUSAGES:

Beef, boerewors, bratwurst, breakfast, black pudding, Cumberland, chipolatas, smoked pork, gluten free, haggis, herb garden, merguez, oriental, pork, peri-peri, smoked beef, tomato, turkey, Toulouse, venison.

Pork with Tomato & Chilli

Heal Farm
Kings Nympton
Umberleigh
Devon EX37 9TB

Tel: 0769 574341

Meat content: 80%

Hardly Mr Average. Closer to our Continental cousins. Solid, coarse ground pork base zapped with tomato and chilli, garlic and something green.

COMMENTS:

'Good for barbecues.'

'Here's a change. Firm. Quite fiery.'

'A red sausage? But nice. Peppery. Quite dry.'

'Too garlicky.'

'Is this what we joined the Common Market for?'

OTHER SAUSAGES:

Plain pork, pork chipolatas, pork with herbs, pork with garlic, smoked garlic, breakfast, Cumberland, venison & bacon, beef, ham poaching, lamb with fresh coriander.

Traditional Pork

McCartney's Family Butchers
56–58 Main Street
Moira
Co. Down
Northern Ireland

Tel: 0846 611422

Meat content: 82%

A handsome, strapping fellow, sort of broad in the shoulder and broader in the hip. No frills or fancy spicing, but good and meaty. A bit heavy on the salt, perhaps.

COMMENTS:

'Very flavoursome.'

'A bit "Oxo-y". '

'Too salty, but otherwise a good all-round product.'

'A bit dry.'

OTHER SAUSAGES:

Low fat pork, bratwurst, thick pork, Olde Time pork, Cumberland, pork with garlic, pork with leek, Italian style, pork with herbs, pork cocktail, Lincolnshire, pork with chives, Indian style, country herb & walnut, pork with banana, mild traditional pork, lamb with mint, traditional beef, mild traditional beef, beef with vegetables, beef with tomato & onion, beef with garlic, curry flavoured beef, beef & pepper.

Rare Breed Pork

Belwood Bros
Booze Wood
Baldersdale
Cotherstone
Barnard Castle
Co. Durham

Tel: 0833 50690

Meat content: 100%

From happy, healthy pigs. Notable texture. Not quite so notable flavour. Good jaw exercise.

COMMENTS:

'Juicy and nicely chewy.'

'Skin is chewy. Rather lumpy.'

'Nice flavour. Rather fatty.'

OTHER SAUSAGES:

Pork.

Farmers' Pork

A. Crombie & Son
97–101 Broughton Street
Edinburgh EH1 3RZ

Tel: 031 556 7643

Meat content: 90%

Mighty, meaty, porky. Which is a bit odd. Beef is supposed to be the classic Scottish farmers' choice. Still, if you need a sausage in the land of the mountain and the flood, this coarse cut number should do the trick.

COMMENTS:

'Great chunky texture.'

'Bit of all right.'

'Good, meaty flavour.'

'Well balanced spices. Quite peppery.'

OTHER SAUSAGES:

Traditional beef, pork, low fat pork, low fat beef, pork & apple, herby pork, gypsy, Cajun, beef & tomato, Larne, savory slicing, Cumberland, Auld Reekie (smoked flavour), Bratwurst.

Best Pork (Traditional, medium Richardson Recipe)

F. Richardson
66 High Street
Brightlingsea
Essex CO7 0AQ

Tel: 0206 302259

Meat content: 70%

Short, dark and plump, not unlike a successful Greek shipowner. A soft touch, and maybe a touch soft for real class. But tasty all the same, and seductively spiced.

COMMENTS:

'A very pleasant sausage.'

'Soft – and very tasty for supper, but perhaps a bit spicy for breakfast.'

'Short, fat, soft.'

OTHER SAUSAGES:

Extra spicy pork, beef, extra spicy beef, lamb & mint.

Beef Links

Andrew Gillespie
1601 Great Western Road
Anniesland X
Glasgow

Tel: 041 959 2015

Meat content: 75%

Scottish classic, i.e. beef all through, coarsely ground. It makes for a dryer mouthful. You may need to get to know this sausage, but it develops splendidly on acquaintance. Salt cries out for ketchup. Or mustard?

COMMENTS:

'Flavour comes out late. Slightly saltier than I like. Texture pleasant.'

'Too salty. Improved with chewing.'

'Pleasant.'

'Too salty. Slightly dry.'

OTHER SAUSAGES:

Pork links, Italian, Cumberland, pork & herbs, beef & garlic, 100% beef links, 100% pork links, Aberdeen Angus links, venison.

Pork, Cider & Apple

Tetbury Traditional Meats
31 Church Street
Tetbury
Glos.

Tel: 0666 502892

Meat content: 65%

For those looking for a balanced diet. A meal in a mouthful. Apple for sweetness, cider for moisture, measured to a no-nonsense, straight-talking basic meatiness.

COMMENTS:

'Succulent. Fairly interesting, salty flavour.'

'Sweet'

'Very good.'

'Juicy but a little salty.'

'Tasty, tasty.'

OTHER SAUSAGES:

Traditional pork, mild pork, smoked pork, pork & cheese, Toulouse, low fat royale, pork & leek, pork & vegetable & garlic, spicy beef, merguez, farmers, ham & apricot, venison & pork.

Toulouse

John Pettit & Sons
33–35 Bethlehem Street
Grimsby
South Humberside

Tel: 0472 349915

Meat content: 80%

No need to cross the Channel for saucisse sorcery. Fine version of the French masterpiece. Fine ground, pepper and garlic nicely balanced.

COMMENTS:

'Very good appearance, particularly the skin.'

'Best yet, and that's not just in comparison with the run of rubbish. Good smooth meat and lovely bit of garlic to lift the taste.'

'Smooth texture. Excellent garlicky taste.'

'Very pleasant indeed.'

OTHER SAUSAGES:

Lincolnshire pork, London pork, Cumberland pork, Lorne, pork & ham, spicy lamb, Aberdeen Angus steak & Guinness, Somerset pork – cider & apple, London beef, lamb & apricot.

Italian Pork

Allan Gardner
16 High Street
Ludgershall
Nr Andover
Hants SP11 9PZ

Tel: 0264 790318

Meat content: 83%

A serious contender. Handsome to the eye and the tongue. Loosish texture. Well fennelled. If you like aniseed balls, you'll love this.

COMMENTS:

'Looks like a sausage should – just asking to be eaten.'

'Aniseed flavour of strong individuality.'

'Nice looking and good flavour.'

'Salient aniseed. Skin rubbery.'

'Good size and shape. Interesting colour and spicy taste.'

OTHER SAUSAGES:

Supreme champion pork, farmhouse, country pork, herb, Lincoln, Cumberland, garlic & herbs, garlic & tomato, Italian style, cowboys, pork & leek, pork & onion, pork & apple, tandoori, barbecue, chilli, sweet 'n' sour, peppered pork, Black Friars, Hawaiian, beef,

beef & tomato, beef curry, gammon & pineapple, venison, lamb & mint, poachers, chicken & ham.

Sausages made to order. Minimum order: 10lbs

Hot & Spicy

Dennis Putt Butchers
194 Watford Road
Croxley Green
Rickmansworth
Herts WD3 3DB

Tel: 0923 221669

Meat content: 75%

Well, it lives up to its name. No chilli overkill, but a sparky number, with enough meatiness and texture to hold up.

COMMENTS:

'Strong peppery aftertaste.'

'Pleasant but peppery.'

'Garlicky and spicy. Nicely controlled even if texture better than flavour.'

'Questionnable skin.'

OTHER SAUSAGES:

Croxley (pork & sage), pork & apple, pork & herb, chilli & garlic, bacon & egg, pork & leek, Cumberland, old fashioned bangers, lamb & mint, beef & tomatoes, beef, pork & chives, pork & peppers, beef & celery, gluten free.

Pork & Chives

Marchants Butchers
Westview
The Street
Bethersden
Nr Ashford
Kent TN26 3AD

Tel: 0233 820224

Meat content: 80–85%

On top of old Smoky, as the song goes, although nothing in the name gives a clue to the flavour. An agreeable change, as the panel agreed. And a good sausage to boot.

COMMENTS:

'This would be a nice breakfast sausage.'

'Slightly smoky. (Why not more really smoked sausages?) Mmmm. Quite nice.'

'Mild smoky ambience.'

OTHER SAUSAGES:

Pork & sage.

Plain Pork

Clifford Bateson
70 Main Street
Hornby
Lancaster

Tel: 05242 21248

Meat content: 70%

Basic instincts say yes, I will have another. A basic sausage with basic virtues. Medium ground meat, pleasantly flavoured.

COMMENTS:

'Sufficient but not overpowering flavour. Even texture. Would make a good meal.'

'A good average sausage. Still a bit salty.'

'Size of mince excellent. Not too big, chewy, not soft.'

OTHER SAUSAGES:

Cumberland, Lincoln, pork & chives, pork & celery, pork & chestnut, Provençal, pork & garlic, pork & country herbs, pork & peppers, pork & pineapple, pork & honey & spice, pork & leek, pork & tomato, pork & apple.

Additive Free Pork & Herbs

Cowman's Famous Sausage Shop
13 Castle Street
Clitheroe
Lancs BB7 2BT

Tel: 0200 23842

Meat content: 75%

The Legend of Lancashire. A real looker. Flavour not up to appearance. Pepper and herbs a bit out of control. Nice, dense, dry texture.

COMMENTS:

'I like pepper but I don't think everyone does. The herbs are a bit unsubtle (unless this was the effect of the Jammy Dodger that I had just prior to judging).'

'Herby flavour masked a bland sausage.'

'Nice and herby – not overherbed, but lacking subtlety of some herby sausages. Looks better than it actually is.'

OTHER SAUSAGES:

Cowman's list over forty varieties of sausage.

Walkers Traditional Pork

Walker & Son (Leicester) Ltd
200 Madeline Road
Burson Industrial Estate
Beaumont Leys
Leicester LE4 1EX

Tel: 0553 340033

Meat content: 75%

A chipolata, and a decent, upstanding member of the congregation. Too soft for greatness, but one to sling alongside the turkey or the roast chicken if you're a died-in-the-wool traditionalist.

COMMENTS:

'Nicely balanced texture. A good middle-of-the-road sausage, if a little on the thin side.'

'Not too bad. Salty. Good texture if on the soft side.'

'A tasty, pleasant sausage suitable for a sandwich on a cold day.'

'Not brilliant.'

OTHER SAUSAGES:

Thick and thin standard pork, Cumberland, Lincolnshire.

Farmhouse Pork

A.W. Curtis
Long Leys Road
Lincoln LN1 1DX

Tel: 0522 527212

Meat content: 70%

It's soft on you, and a bit on the herbaceous border side but, if that's the kind of sausage you like, then you'll like this one. Rather a personal sausage, I'd say.

COMMENTS:

'Rather sweet. Could be served with mint icecream for desert.'

'A fireside sausage worthy of a good claret and brown bread.'

'Over spiced. No meat flavour. Very loose texture.'

'Very herby. Not too salty.'

'Very tasty. Just the right flavour.'

'Good. Wholesome. Slightly bland.'

OTHER SAUSAGES:

Lincolnshire, Lincolnshire chipolatas, pork & chives, pork & tomato, pork & apple.

Lincolnshire Pork

John Swepstone
28 High Street
Holbeach
Spalding
Lincs PE12

Tel: 0406 23283

Meat content: 80%

Of the crumbling tendency, but a happy snagger nonetheless. Excellent balance of spice and pepper brings meat to the fore. Unmarred by horrid herbs.

COMMENTS:

'Very meaty. Pleasantly coarse. Slightly retentive skin.'

'Good meaty texture.'

'Very nice flavour – plenty of pork, but lack of substance let it down.'

'A very encouraging starter with rich flavour.'

'Excellent, peppery, robust. Slightly greasy.'

Dalesman Pork

J. Warburton
493 Rice Lane
Aintree
Liverpool 9
L9 8AP

Tel: 051 525 2610

Meat content: 70%

One for the hills as well as the dales. Something to get
your teeth into (if you can! See below). But once you
have, it won't let go. Chunky cut.

COMMENTS:

'Tough skin. Well rounded. Could be lingered over.'

'Well balanced.'

'Very strong skin. Rather chewy.'

'Thick skinned albeit tasty. A good balance between
wet and dry.'

OTHER SAUSAGES:

Farmhouse, spicy garlic, pork & tomato, Cumberland,
traditional pork, traditional beef.

Californian Pork

Frank Godfrey Ltd
7 Highbury Barn
London N5

Tel: 071 226 2425

Meat content: 75%

Red and green peppers, coriander and mustard – quite
what these have to do with California I don't know.
Quite smooth on the tongue. As good looking as a
Californian with rather more personality.

COMMENTS:

'Individual sweet pepper taste. Disturbing tactility,
smooth with the rough.'

'Marred by split skins, but quite distinctive pepper
flavour.'

'Colourful, but pleasant flavour.'

OTHER SAUSAGES:

Directors pork, pork & leek, Lincolnshire country,
venison with sherry & pork, beef & tomato with Worcester sauce.

Smoked Pork, Tomato & Chive

Postons Butchers
262 Hoe Street
Walthamstow
London E17

Tel: 081 520 3300

Meat content: 75%

One for the more daring sausage lover. Perhaps not an every day sausage, but with all the right qualities – character, flavour and fine cut texture.

COMMENTS:

'Frankfurter type flavour; again well spiced. Skins fairly tough.'

'Strong, rich flavour. Excellent colour. A little over garlicked.'

'Looks exciting. Strong "foreign" smell. Skin a bit everlasting. Good texture. Good to spice up your Sunday.'

OTHER SAUSAGES:

Scotch beef, honey roast pork, Italian tomato, Cumberland, Essex country, Lincoln, Cambridge stout, pork scrumpy, oak & hickory smoked, pork & garlic, venison royale, hot 'n' spicy lamb, boerewors, merguez, Toulouse, bratwurst, and others.

Traditional Pork

Richardson
110 South Ealing Road
London W5

Tel: 081 567 4405

Meat content: 75%

King of the breakfast table and more interesting than
the newspaper. Well balanced spicing. No intrusive
herbs. Medium fine mince. A splendid match for tomato
ketchup.

COMMENTS:

'My gran would love this sausage.'

'Good flavour. Nicely porky.'

'I think I'll have a second helping.'

'Neither one thing, nor the other.'

'Soft and squidgy, but quite pleasant.'

OTHER SAUSAGES:

Pork & leek, lamb & leek, beef, Cumberland, Lincolnshire, pork chipolatas.

Thick Pork

Graham Eyes High Class Butcher
17 Wesley Street
Southport
Merseyside

Tel: 0704 532481

Meat content: 70%

An Ian Botham among sausages, i.e. a fine all-rounder. Nothing fancy, but solid and meaty. A bit salty for some tastes. Excellent texture.

COMMENTS:

'An excellent, ordinary sausage.'

'Pleasant – slightly too salty. But fair as a general sort of sausage.'

'Very good. Meaty.'

'Could do with a little less salt, and some, just a little, seasoning.'

OTHER SAUSAGES:

Thin pork, Cumberland, pork & leek, pork & pepper, pork & apple & cider, pork & cheese & onion, mild curried pork, beef & beer, venison & red wine, lamb & mint & rosemary, pork & tomato & smoked bacon, Lincolnshire, low-fat pork & onion (95% lean meat), ham & pineapple.

Best Pork

Muffs of Bromborough
3–5 Allport Lane
Bromborough
Wirral
Merseyside L62 7HH

Tel: 051 334 2002

Meat content: 85%

Something to keep for yourself. Short, or rather slender (chipolata sized) on looks, long on flavour, sound on texture and with a little touch of originality, too. Read on.

COMMENTS:

'A good example of what a sausage should be. Pity about the appearance.'

'Citrusy.'

'Real sausage smell. Hint of lemon. Manageable size.'

'Things are looking up. I am biased towards thin sausages, but this should satisfy the strongest faddist. Really tasty with a tang of lemon.'

OTHER SAUSAGES:

Cumberland, pure beef, huntsman.

Pork

Wright's Butchers
129 Constitution Hill
Old Catton
Norwich
Norfolk NR6 7RN

Tel: 0603 408319

Meat content: 85%

The Old Colonel. Quite peppery and crumbly, but good at heart. Quite highly spiced, in fact, but not so as to come between the pork and the tastebuds. Good flavour.

COMMENTS:

'Stimulates the tastebuds nourished by years of curry.'

'An interesting and satisfying taste without undue distinction.'

'Slightly too "Walls". A bit pink though an excellent afterglow.'

'Packed with meatiness.'

'Strong spicy flavour.'

'Slightly overspiced.'

OTHER SAUSAGES:

Beef, beef & lamb.

Pork with Sage

Hutton & Smith
48 Main Street
Burton Joyce
Nottingham NG14 5DZ

Tel: 0602 312133

Meat content: 70%

A bit of a smoothie. Well balanced. Sweetness of pork
not overwhelmed by sage. Fine texture. A bit short on
character. You want to make further acquaintance even
if you're not quite sure why.

COMMENTS:

'Good healthy appearance with an invitation to a
further bite.'

'Nice and meaty but slightly bland.'

'Straight, fat, well balanced.'

'Very smooth texture.'

'Neither batter nor bowler. Not spicy enough.'

'Quite without flavour. Steve Davis lives on them.'

'Good average sausage.'

OTHER SAUSAGES:

Thick plain pork, thin plain pork, game (when in
season).

English Pork & Sage

Mrs Elizabeth King Ltd
Hardigate Road
Crodwell Butler
Nottingham NG12 3AG

Tel: 0602 332252

Meat content: 85%

A modest, retiring example of its tribe. You almost think 'Where is it?' and then the flavour comes through, sweet and charming. Balanced, unassertive spice. Slightly crumbly in the mouth.

COMMENTS:

'A sausage for all seasons.'

'Nondescript. Suitable for John Major's breakfast table.'

'Good tasty herb sausage. Not overpowering.'

'Chunky texture.'

'Nice flavour and texture.'

'Very encouraging.'

'Very herby. Rather coarse.'

OTHER SAUSAGES:

Nottinghamshire, pork tomato, & sage, mild.

Pork

A.B. Bosley & Son
13 Oxford Road
Abingdon
Oxon OX14 2ED

Tel: 0235 520258

Meat content: 70%

High wire act. Superb balance between seasoning and meat, so there's plenty of pork flavour. Nicely ground too, not too dense, not too crumbly.

COMMENTS:

'Tasty, tasty, very, very tasty.'

'Not too bad. A bit on the soft side.'

'It'd do, but I'm not wild about it.'

'Nice looking. Nice eating.'

'Quite fine texture.'

OTHER SAUSAGES:

Country pork, lamb & mint, traditional beef, pork chipolatas.

Special Pork

Gabriel Machin
7 Market Place
Henley-on-Thames
Oxon RG9 2AA

Tel: 0491 574377

Meat content: 70%

A good, middle-of-the-road, sausage for all seasons sort
of sausage. Quite peppery, but not so as to mask the
flavour of the coarse ground meat.

COMMENTS:

'A bit on the crumbly side.'

'Inoffensive. Quite likeable in fact. On the peppery
side.'

'A breakfast sausage. Not enough to it for supper.'

'Not too meaty. Or perhaps not meaty enough. Can't
quite make up my mind.'

OTHER SAUSAGES:

Ordinary pork, Cumberland, beef, gluten free.

Country Fayre Pork & Chives

John Walton Butchers
The Butcher's Shop
South Side
Steeple Aston
Bicester
Oxon

Tel: 0869 40222

Meat content: 80%

One of those oh-yes-I'll-have-some-of-that-sausages.
Cries out to be eaten. Subtly flavoured, perhaps even a
little over-subtle. Firm, moist texture. Sound all-
rounder.

COMMENTS:

'Mild flavour but pleasant.'

'Looked great.'

'Subtle, definite flavour. Fatty, good texture. Very
Good.'

OTHER SAUSAGES:

Ham & tomato, spicy pork, lamb & mint, Lincolnshire
pork, honey roast pork, beef, golden rose pork, pork &
garlic.

Plain Pork

Roney's
276 Sharrow Vale Road
Sheffield S11 8ZH

Tel: 0742 660593

Meat content: 85%

Most people would be very happy to find this on their plates. An endearing banger, with well rounded qualities. Feast for eye as well as gob.

COMMENTS:

'Good.'

'Very good.'

'Best so far as a regular banger.'

'Very pleasant. All purpose.'

'Too pale in colour. Skin too chewy.'

OTHER SAUSAGES:

Pork & leek, pork & tomato.

Pork

C.E. Wells
14 The Square
Clun
Shropshire

Tel:

Meat content: 75%

Rather appealing. In the minor key, but a good platefull all the same. The natural sweetness of the fine minced pork gives this fellow its quality. Minimalist seasoning.

COMMENTS:

'Quite sweet. Nice flavour.'

'A sausage you could take home to mother.'

'What happened to the flavour?'

'Good for cocktails rather than a serious feed.'

OTHER SAUSAGES:

Lincolnshire, Cumberland.

Royal

A.W. Lashford & Son
18 St John's Way
Knowle
Solihull
West Midlands B93 0LE
(Available at four shops in Solihull and many outlets in
the West Midlands.)

Tel: 0564 775808

Meat content: 82%

Fuel for the inner man and woman. A fine, meaty, solid
Midlands sausage. Quite dense in texture. Perhaps a
little salty for some tastes. A hint of frankfurter about
the flavour.

COMMENTS:

'I like this but I can't state exactly why.'

'Good sausage.'

'Over-chewy. Needs mustard.'

'A most unusual flavour. Tasty, but a little salty.'

'Brilliant spice.'

'Smoky taste. Attractive to firemen and kipper lovers.'

'Tasty and meaty.'

OTHER SAUSAGES:

Pork apple & leek, beef & garlic, Carlton (Guinness
kidney & mushroom), pork sage & other herbs, lamb &
apricot, venison.

100% Pure Pork

Salters Family Butchers
107–109 High Street
Aldeburgh
Suffolk IP15 5AR

Tel: 0728 452758

Meat content: 100%

Small is beautiful, less is more, *multum in parvo*, etc. Undeniably on the small side but, like Dudley Moore, charming, packed with talent, and you want a second helping.

COMMENTS:

'A good, little sausage.'

'Poor looking, but very tasty.'

'Short. Thin. Poor looking. Neutral taste.'

OTHER SAUSAGES:

Aldeburgh pork special, Salters' savoury, pork chipolatas.

Country Style Pork

Bushell's Farm Shop
1 Little Woodcote Estate
Woodmansterne Road
Carshalton
Surrey SM5 4AL

Tel: 081 643 1600

Meat content: 75%

A fine, fat chap. Homely, agreeable, pleasant. Short on fireworks. A kindly uncle sort of sausage.

COMMENTS:

'Nice one.'

'Excellent breakfast and barbecue sausage.'

'A very nice sausage.'

'Excellent breakfast sausage.'

'Good shape, nicely curved with good bobbly ends, but sadly a bit bland.'

OTHER SAUSAGES:

Pork & leek, pork & sage, pork & garlic, plain pork, special (preservative free) chipolata.

FINALIST

Garlic Pork

Collins Butchers
Collins Court
High Street
Cranleigh
Surrey GU6 8AS

Tel: 0483 274123

Meat content: 80%

Ginger & Fred, M&S, Gilbert & Sullivan, garlic &
pork. It's funny how garlic seems to suit pork. This
fellow was no exception. Firm to the tooth, sweet to the
tongue. Quite finely cut.

COMMENTS:

'Nicely balanced garlicky flavour.'

'Strong garlic. Good meat. Good sausage – I would
not buy it though.'

'A good strong flavour takes the garlic.'

OTHER SAUSAGES:

Pork.

Welsh Leek

Lindy's Gourmet Foods
30 Croydon Road
Caterham
Surrey CR3 6QB

Tel: 0883 341 719

Meat content: 75%

An Honorable, rather than a Lord or above. Good, if
not quite top drawer. A useful sausage to have about.
Particularly if you like leeks. Low on fat, too, if dryness
is anything to go by. Coarse cut.

COMMENTS:

'A little dry – but a good standard herby taste.'

'A fairly average herby sausage.'

'Quite dry and coarse in texture.'

OTHER SAUSAGES:

Lindy's make over thirty-one different sausages. This is
a selection of some: Lindy's traditional, Szechuan pork,
pork bananza, Mexican Pedro, pork Salonika, lamb
Riviera, merguez, beef madras, steak & kidney, gamek-
eeper's choice, turkey supreme, boerewors.

Traditional Pork & Sage

Gibson & Coe
49 George Street
Hove
East Sussex BN3 5LX

Tel: 0273 731407

Meat content: 74%

Won't set the world, or the mouth, on fire, but easy to get along with. No rough edges. Properly chewy and moist. Splendid vehicle for ketchup.

COMMENTS:

'Pleasantly herby. Slightly soapy.'

'A little bland but distinctly edible.'

OTHER SAUSAGES:

Traditional beef, spicy Italian, pork & garlic, lamb & mint, pork & leek, smoky barbecue pork.

Italian

Goodies
Stall 18b
Swansea Market
Oxford Street
Swansea

Tel: 0792 456250

Meat content: 90%

Herbalist's dream. Big flavour. Prominently peppered.
Lots of lean meat. Dry tendencies. Packs a punch.

COMMENTS:

'Deliciously spicy. Great texture.'

'Strong flavour. Too strong for my taste. And some
gristle.'

'Overdoes the pepper. Interesting and exotic – but one
would not like to eat a lot. It's good for a tasting.'

'Nice flavour. Good use of pepper.'

OTHER SAUSAGES:

Pork & chilli, lean pork, lean pork with garlic & oregano, pork & cider, pork & beer, boerewors, merguez.

Pork

I.D. Newman & Son
8 Church Street
Melksham
Wiltshire

Tel: 0225 703386

Meat content: 75%

A handsome, upright, hunky chap. A sausage you wouldn't mind being seen with. Firm texture. A touch of bite and a distinctly porky flavour.

COMMENTS:

'Good flavour and texture.'

'Good appearance. Tasty.'

'Slightly sour taste.'

OTHER SAUSAGES:

Beef, beef & Guinness, beef additive free, pork savoury, lamb & mint, pork savoury, chipolatas, pork & tomato, pork & curry, pork & apple, pork & garlic, additive free pork, pork chipolatas with herbs, pork & baked beans, Cumberland, pork & pineapple.

Pork & Leek

Alan Bennett Ltd
100 High Street
Wednesfield
Wolverhampton WV11 1SZ

Tel: 0902 732750

Meat content: 75%

Cooked properly, this thoroughly decent sausage should please anyone who likes their sausages to play it straight. The leeks give a hint of sweetness, and the texture is even and firm. A good sausage to reintroduce you to the world at breakfast.

COMMENTS:

'Good pork flavour enlivened by a hint of pepperiness.'

'A top-notch traditional sausage.'

'Exemplary use of flavouring.'

'Not solid or chewy enough for a die-hard sausage lover.'

'Not one that really stands out in a tasting session, but I'd be happy to see it at breakfast.'

OTHER SAUSAGES:

Pork & chive, pork & garlic, pork & apple, pork & tomato, extra lean pork, plain pork (65%), Cumberland, traditional beef, venison.

Chunky Pork & Chopped Leek

Boxley's
Windmill Bank
Wombourne
Nr. Wolverhampton WV5 9JD.

Tel: 0902 892359

Meat content: 70%

The Beauty, but not the Beast. Lovely to look at, fine to nibble, but a bit short on final oomph. Leek not really in evidence. Compact, fine cut texture, and a juicy mouthful.

COMMENTS:

'Chewy.'

'Good product. Very tasty.'

'Very strong texture. Would make a superb casserole sausage.'

'Very good.'

'Dull. A sausage for the lover of supermarket beefburgers.'

OTHER SAUSAGES:

Gluten free prime pork, Gold Medal, pork with sage & herbs, pork with tomatoes, pork with apple & onion, pork with banana, beef, beef with tomato, beef with horseradish, beef with garlic & tomato, Sicilian, beef with Bass ale & mustard, Gornal super smokies (German).

Spicy

Robbins
35 Port Street
Evesham
Worcs WR11 6AD

Tel: 0386 446161

Meat content: 85%

Very well behaved, and good looking with it. Wholesome and handsome, coarse cut with politely meaty flavour. Didn't quite hold together when cut up. A touch too much bread or rusk?

COMMENTS:

'A proper meaty sausage and a good looker.'

'Good. Wholesome.'

'Texture too coarse.'

'A sausage to take home to mother.'

'Worth the visit, but not the diversion.'

'Great appearance. Positive flavour.'

OTHER SAUSAGES:

Standard pork, beef & tomato, pork & chive, lamb & mint, Cumberland.

Pork

F.P. Caselli
3A Whinney Moor Avenue
Wakefield
West Yorkshire WF2 8RF

Tel: 0924 374313

Meat content: 85%

A pillar of the pork sausage establishment. Good meat. Good seasoning. Good eating.

COMMENTS:

'A good, strong and lasting flavour. Lovely skin.'

'Excellent, well balanced sausage. Best yet. Uncomplicated and unpretentious.'

'Unappealing in cross section. Smells very good.'

OTHER SAUSAGES:

Pork & garlic, wild boar, venison, Guinness, lamb with fresh herbs, Lincolnshire, Yorkshire, Cumberland, beef with Scottish seasoning, thin pork, thick pork, thin beef, thick beef, thin tomato, thick tomato.

Butchers' Style Pork

Safeway
Safeway stores
Nationwide

Meat content: 85%

Here's a turn up for the books. Really rather good. Broad in its appeal, rather than quirky and individual. Solid and meaty, and spiced with good manners. A well-cut three-piece-grey-suit sausage.

COMMENTS:

'Smoky flavour. (Scout camp fire.)'

'Good looking – and good. Slightly smoky flavour.'

'Another campside sausage, this time with flavour.'

'Forgettable.'

Readers' Recommendations

In alphabetical order of county/city.

Roseden Farm Shop
Roseden
Wooperton
Alnwick

The Real Meat Company
7 Hayes Place
Bear Flat
Bath
Avonshire

Vitello D'Oro
Ford End Road
Queens Park
Bedford
Bedfordshire

Mr J King
John King Butcher
The Street
Shurlock Row
Berkshire

W Vicars
W Vicars & Son
20 West Street
Reading
Berkshire

G Millhouse
G Millhouse
12–14 The Mall
Clifton
Bristol
BS8 4DS

Mr P Noble
A Edwards & Sons
Uptown House
High Street Vatton
Bristol

Mr R Barrett
R Barretts Butcher
High Street
Bailsham
Cambridge
Cambridgeshire

Mr S J Bull
S J Bull and Son
13 High Street
Waterbeach
Cambridge
Cambridgeshire

Mr Leach
Leach Butchers
Melbourn
Cambridgeshire

Naturally Yours
The Horse and Gate
Witchum Toll
Ely
Cambridgeshire

Mr F Gorno
Frank Gorno
30 Tudor Street
Cardiff

Parsons Butcher
34 Fishguard Road
Llanishen
Cardiff

Mr A J Boon
A J Boon Butchers
Knutsford Road
Chelford
Nr Macclesfield
Cheshire

C Green
C Green
38 Palmeston Street
Bollington
Nr Macclesfield
Cheshire

W Lindsey
W Lindsey Butchers
High Street
Cockermouth
Cumbria

Mr C Middlehurst
Colin Middlehurst
St John's Market
Town Hall Square
Widnes
Cheshire

Mr B Walton
Bill Walton
Alderley Road
Alderley Edge
Cheshire

Wibbs
Witton Street
Northwich
Cheshire

H Newbould
H Newbould Ltd Food Manufacturers
Startforth Road
Riverside Park Industrial Estate
Middlesborough
Cleveland

Twizzells Sausages
Gilly Flatts Farm
Bishopton
Stockton-on-Tees
Cleveland

Mr H Jones
Merrivale Foods
The Level
Cowstantine
Falmouth
Cornwall
TR11 5PU

W Bateman
W Bateman & Son Butchers Shop
Whitecroft
Gosforth
Seascale
Cumbria
CA20

W Bewley
W Bewley Butcher
West View
Main Street Bootle Street
Millom
Cumbria

K R Richardson
Blackstocks
Market Square
Alston
Cumbria

Mr R Flett
Rodney Flett
St Johns Precinct
Workington
Cumbria

Mr J Hayton
John Hayton
Main Street
Stoveley
Cumbria

Myers of Keswick
Station Street
Keswick
Cumbria

Mr H Goldsack
**Don Richardson's Pork
Butchers**
Senhouse Street
Maryport
Cumbria

Mr M Slack
Michael Slack
Newlands Farm
Raisebeck Tabay
Penrith
Cumbria

**The Ullswater Meat
Company**
Ullswater Road
Penrith
Cumbria
CA11 7EA

**The Chatsworth Estate
Farm**
Pilsley
Derbyshire

Arthur's
67 Fore Street
Topsham
Devon

W F Chinn
W F Chinn
Marsh Lane
Crediton
Devon

Cox the Butcher
High Street
Crediton
Devon

D J Haggett
D J Haggett
2 New Court Road
Silverton
Exeter
Devon

W H Luke
**W H Luke & Son Ltd
Meat Product
Manufacturers**
Endsleigh Road
Preston
Plymouth
Devon

Redfern's Butchers
Teignmouth
Devon

Riverford Farm Shop
Staverton
Devon
TQ9 6AF

R J Balson
R J Balson
9 West Allington
Bridport
Dorset

Bon Appetite
3 Frederick Place
Weymouth
Dorset

Howells
16 Church Street
Lyme Regis
Dorset
D17 3DB

Hollands (Butchers)
Princes Street
Dorchester
Dorset

The Sausage Shop
Dairy House
Wigbeth Farm
Horton
Wimborne
Dorset
BH21 7JH

Mr J Keenan
John Keenan
The Market Place
Wolsingham
Co Durham

K Tarn
K Tarn & Sons
Horsemarket
Barnard Castle
Co. Durham

D Matthews
Dai Matthews
Stone Street
Llandovery
Dyfed

Mr G Bower
Bowers of Stockbridge
75 Raeburn Place
Edinburgh
EH4 1JG

Mr J Frindlay
Frindlay's of Portobello
116 Portobello High
Street
Edinburgh
EH15 1AL

Mr C C Hornig
Chas C Hornig & Son
47 South Clerk Street
Edinburgh
EH8

Archers
7 Moulsham Street
Chelmsford
Essex
CM2 0HR

Mr J Butcher
J Butcher
(Family Butcher)
100 The Street
Little Waltham
Essex
CM3 3NI

Mr J Carter
Carters
The Square
Stock
Ingatestone
Essex

Church (Pork Butchers)
Ltd
224 High Street
Epping
Essex
CM16 4AG

Co-op
Gloucester Avenue
Moulsham Lodge
Chelmsford
Essex

Harvey's Sausages
Unit 10
Chelmsford Road
Great Dunmow
Essex
CM6 1HD

Mr I Kerridge
Kerridge's Butchers
9 Court Street
Nayland
Colchester
Essex

Mr M A King
**M A King Family
Butchers**
121 Frinton Road
Holland-on-Sea
Essex
CO15 5UP

F J Martin
F J Martin
72 Canterbury Road
Colchester
Essex

Smiths
Woodfield Road
Hadleigh
Essex

Sweetlands Butchers
Stortford Road
Great Dunmow
Essex

Mr J Williams
John Williams
High Road
Benfleet
Essex

Mr J Cockburn
**James Buckburn Master
Butchers**
Market Street
Galashiels

Fawcetts of Richmond
Metrocentre
Gateshead

Mr J Hughes
John Hughes
1 Hendre Road
The Square
Pencoed
Mid Glamorgan

R Hale
R Hale
8 King Street
Stroud
Gloucestershire

Mr P Hanley
Peter Hanley
5 London Road
Tetbury
Gloucestershire
GL8 8JQ

Harris Butcher
78 Westgate Street
Gloucester
Gloucestershire

Mr K Harris
Keith Harris Butcher
Bishops Walk
Cirencester
Gloucestershire

Holpins
Salter Street
Berkeley
Gloucestershire

Mr R Pitt
Reg Pitt
160 Bath Road
Cheltenham
Gloucestershire

Roberts Butchers
Port Diarwic
Gwynedd

Mr D Bowtell
David Bowtell
Home Farm Shop
East Tisted
Alton
Hampshire
GU34 3QJ

Mr G David
M & G David Family
Butchers
High Street
Hartley Wintney
Hampshire

Mr Gates
Mr Gates Village Butcher
The Green
Milford on Sea
Lymington
Hampshire

Mr B Gibson
Gibsons
Charter Place
Watford Market
Watford
Hertfordshire

S W Pickles
S W Pickles & Son High-
Class Family Butchers
3 Fernhill Lane
New Milton
Hampshire
BH25 5JN

L J Smith
L J Smith
3 Riverside
Bishopstoke
Eastleigh
Hampshire

Sutherlands of Eldon Ltd
Upper Eldon
King's Somborne
Hampshire

H H Treagust
H H Treagust & Sons
17 High Street
Emsworth
Hampshire

Hurley's
16 Drapers Lane
Leominster
Herefordshire
HR6 8ND

Mr W R Turner
Billy's Family Butcher
92 Haldens
Welwyn Garden City
Hertfordshire
AD7 1DD

Mr J Gregory
J Gregory
(Family Butcher)
Cheddington Road
Long Marston
Nr Tring
Hertfordshire

Mr J Robertson
I G Robertson & Son
Stoneycroft
Warners End
Hemel Hempstead
Hertfordshire

Mr C White
The Butchers
Braughing
Nr Ware
Hertfordshire

Smiths of High Street
94 High Street
Barton Upon Humber
South Humberside

Mr R Conelly
Roy Conelly
50 Twydall Green
Gillingham
Kent

S W Doughty
S W Doughty Butchers
The Street
Doddington
Sittingbourne
Kent

Mr M Edwards
Mark & Sons
The Butchers Shop
The Greet Matfield
Tonbridge
Kent
TN12 7JR

Mr A Hargreave
Spar Supermarket
The Parade
Meopham
Kent

Hedger's
25 St Dunstan's Street
Canterbury
Kent
CT2 8BT

Hoads
Rolvenden
Nr Tenterden
Kent

G M Johns
G M Johns
317 Dover Road
Walmer
Deal
Kent
CT14 7NX

Kennedy's
High Street
Bromley
Kent

Mr K Jones
Kevin's Family Butchers
175 Silverdale Road
Tunbridge Wells
Kent

Mr H G Longley
H G Longley Pork
Butcher
49 St Peters Street
Canterbury
Kent

Mr S Mallet
Cable & Keane
24 Sun Street
Canterbury
Kent

M Offen
M Offen
High Street
Shoreham
Kent

Mr D Skinner
Dennis Skinner
Sevenoaks
Kent

Mr B Austin
G H Theobold
99 High Street
Whitstable
Kent
C15 1AV

Mr G Haffner
**George Haffner (Foods)
Ltd**
14 Keirby Walk
Burnley
Lancashire

Mr T Haworth
Cowburn Bros Butchers
39 Granville Road
Blackburn
Lancashire

John's Butchers
32a New Market Place
Bolton
Lancashire

M & R Jones
M J Butchers
12 The Crescent
St Annes
Lytham St Annes
Lancashire

Mr J Nabb
Jim Nabb
346 Walmsley Road
Bury
Lancashire
BL9 6QF

Mr H Trickett
Harry Trickett
719 Bacup Road
Waterfoot
Rossendale
Lancashire
BB4 7EU

A C Wild
40 Warner Street
Accrington
Lancashire

Mr A Bott
Gregory's Butchers
1 Granville Street
Market Harborough
Leicestershire

Mr M F Wood
Michael F Wood
51 Hartopp Road
Leicester
Leicestershire

Adams Port Products Ltd
Spalding
Lincolnshire
PE12 6EZ

T Bycroft
T Bycroft
Wormsgate
Boston
Lincolnshire

C F Jackson
C F Jackson Butcher
118 Eastgate
Louth
Lincolnshire

Mr R Mountain
**Robert Mountain Pork
Butcher**
High Street
Boston
Lincolnshire

Parkinson's
86 Winsover Road
Spalding
Lincolnshire

D F Oswin
Sowerby's
39–40 Sincil Street
Lincoln
Lincolnshire

Topliss Butchers
24 High Street
Kirton in Lindsey
Lincolnshire

Mr D J Thomas
**David J Thomas
(Butcher)**
7 Stepney Precinct
Town Centre
Llanelli

Baron Munich
8 Old Compton Street
London
W1

Biggles
66 Marylebone Lane
London
W1

Mr Buckingham
Buckingham
63 Blythe Road
Brook Green
London
W14

Corrigans
Colney Hatch Lane
Muswell Hill
London

A Dove
A Dove & Son
71 Northcote Road
London
SW11

Eddies
White Horse Lane
Stepney
London
E1

Hearn and Sons
Abbeville Road
Clapham South
London
SW4

Kennedy's Butchers
Camberwell
London

C Lidgate
C Lidgate
Holland Park Road
London
W14

Mackay Bros
Turnham Green Terrace
Chiswick
London
W6

Meat City
507 Smithfield Market
London
EC1

O'Hagans
192 Trafalgar Road
Greenwich
London
SE10

Simply Sausages
Harts Corner Central
Market
341 Farringdon Street
London
EC4

G G Sparkes
G G Sparkes Wholesale
& Retail Butchers
24 Old Dover Road
Blackheath
London
SE3 7BT

Unique Butchers
217 Holloway Road
London
N7 8DL

Chops and Change
Unit 6
Church Lane Arcade
Coleraine
Co. Londonderry

A E Matthews (Butchers)
Ltd
Park Way House
24 Longwood Road
Trafford Park
Manchester
M17 1PZ

Mr P Smethurst
Peter Smethurst
85 Greenleach Lane
Roe Green
Worsley
Nr Manchester

N Whieldon
N Whieldon
5 Queensway
East Didsbury
Manchester
M1

D J Marshall
D J Marshall Family
Butcher
16 Grand Parade
Wembley
Middlesex
HA9 9JS

Mr G Paine
G Paine
416 Alexandra Avenue
Rayners Lane
South Harrow
Middlesex
HA2 9TR

Mr B Pickering
Bryan Pickering
The Street
Old Costessey
Norwich
Norfolk

Mr T Bell
Tony Bell
(Family Butcher)
High Street
Brigstock
Northamptonshire

E H Panter
E H Panter (Butchers)
Ltd
Little Houghton
Northampton
Northamptonshire

Mr R Pryor
Roger Pryor
High Street
Syresham
Northamptonshire

Daybells (Butcher)
Market Place
Newark on Trent
Nottinghamshire

Masters
Victoria Centre Market
Nottingham
Nottinghamshire

W F Payling
W F Payling & Son
Family Butcher
Main Street
Aslockton
Nottinghamshire

B Thompson
B Thompson
361 Mansfield Road
Nottingham
Nottinghamshire

A B Bosley
A B Bosley Butcher
Oxford Road
Abingdon
Oxfordshire

Castle & Sons
High Street
Burford
Oxfordshire

J W Harman
J W Harman & Son
High Street
Milton Under Wychwood
Oxfordshire
OX7 6EW

Slatters
The Butchers Shop
Chipping Norton Road
Chadlington
Oxfordshire
OX7 3NJ

P Thomas
Pat Thomas
Market Square
Faringdon
Oxfordshire

Franks Brothers Butchers
Peterborough

Mr W Jones
William Jones & Sons
1–3 High Street
Newtown
Powys

Halls Butchers
32 Sandygate Road
Crosspool
Sheffield

Mr Kempka
Kempka of Sheffield
352 Abbeydale Road
Sheffield

Mr E Leigh
Edward Leigh
Hickmott Road
Sharrow
Sheffield

Mr J Maron
John Maron
The High Street
Newport
Shropshire

Mr J Marsh
John Marsh
High Street
Newport
Shropshire

Maynards
Weston Under Redcastle
Shropshire

Mr A Towers
A Towers
Frankwell Roundabout
Shrewsbury
Shropshire
SY3 8NW

Mr B Pocock
Barrett Bros
25 Market Street
Crewkerne
Somerset

Ms C Reynolds
Swaddles Green Farm
Hare Lane
Buckland St Mary
Chard
Somerset
TA20 3JR

F J Scriven
F J Scriven & Sons
Fore Street
North Retherton
Somerset

Sharmans
North Street
Martock
Somerset

Mr D Parkins
Dough Parkin
3 Seabank Road
Southport

D Evans
D Evans & Son
40 Bore Street
Lichfield
Staffordshire

Mr R Powner
Browns Pork Butchers
Indoor Market Hall
Newcastle Under Lyme
Staffordshire

F Holloway
F Holloway & Sons
The Rookery
Newmarket
Suffolk

E W Revett
E W Revett
81 High Street
Wickham Market
Woodbridge
Suffolk
IP13

Cravato
36 Mabel Street
Woking
Surrey
GU21 1NW

H J Grimes
**H J Grimes Ltd
(Inc H & J White)**
562 Chessington Road
West Ewell
Surrey
KT19 9HJ

Hatto & Sons
Frimley Road
Camberley
Surrey

Mr B Noel
Noel's Butchers
Dartmouth Avenue
Sheerwater
Woking
Surrey

Canhams
48 Church Road
Hove
East Sussex

A S Fry
Messrs A S Fry Butcher
89 Lingfield Road
East Grinstead
Sussex

W D Hunt Butchers
18 Broadwater Street
West
Worthing
Sussex
BN16 9DA

F Jarvis
F Jarvis & Sons
High Street
Burwash
East Sussex

Old Spot Farm
Piltdown
Nr Uckfield
East Sussex
TN22 3XN

Mr A Woodward
Alan Woodward
High Street
Henfield
West Sussex
BN5

Mr R Thomas
Howard Thomas & Son
1 Frogmore Avenue
Sketty
Swansea
SA2 9DT

Nichollsons
140 Park View
Whitley Bay
Tyne & Wear

L Leonard
L Leonard & Son
210 Walsall Wood Road
Aldridge
Walsall

Mr S Crowe
Steve Crowe Butcher
Whitemoor Road
Kenilworth
Warwickshire

Ms M Bowkett
Maureen Bowkett
686 Wolverhampton
Road
Oldbury
Warley
West Midlands

K Boxal
K Boxal
Straits Road
Lower Gosnal
Dudley
West Midlands

Mr L Walker
Leonard Walker
Market Square
Malmesbury
Wiltshire

Appletons of Ripon
Market Square
Ripon
North Yorkshire
HG4

E G Bullivant
E & G Bullivant
Vicarage Farm
Claxton
York
North Yorkshire

Mr D Gath
Douglas Gath Butcher
6 Cowpasture Road
Ilkley
West Yorkshire

Mr Hey
Mr Hey
Brook Street
Wakefield
Yorkshire

Lofthouse Foods
Lingwell Gate Lane
Lofthouse
Nr Wakefield
Yorkshire
WF3 3JN

J M Robinson
J M Robinson Butcher
Great Smeaton
Northallerton
North Yorkshire
DL6 0RX

The British Sausage
Appreciation Society

Of all the foodstuffs that we as a nation enjoy, there are few – if any – that arouse the same affection, strength of feeling, passion and downright pleasure as the great British sausage.

Around the dinner table, in the pub, at the breakfast café, or in top restaurants, sausages never fail to delight; inspiring the kind of animated discussion on flavour, texture, consistency and taste that must leave foreign observers perplexed.

Of course, there is no such thing as *the* great British sausage: as a nation of sausage aficiandos will testify, there are hundreds of different styles, types and varieties – and each has its loyal group of consumer champions. Indeed, there are upwards of four hundred different British sausages in regular production. Many of the best known, the Cumberlands and Lincolnshires, will also be made by individual butchers to their own unique recipes, which means that you could probably eat a different British sausage every day for ten years. The joy of the banger however, is that few of those would fail to please.

And it is not stretching the case to say that sausages are an inspiration. When the British Sausage Bureau launched a quest for a song in praise of the banger it was besieged with entries. Astonishing heights of creativity were achieved in the crafting by authors in praise of what might appear, to the uninitiated, to be the *humble* British sausage.

But those of us in the know, those of us who share the cravings that only sausages can satisfy, are resolute in the belief that the sausage stands among the mighty; that there is, as one songsmith put it, 'no better way to fill up your plate!'

If you share these sentiments and would like to join fellow enthusiasts in the British Sausage Appreciation

Society, please write to us for further information at the address below:

British Sausage Appreciation Society
26 Fitzroy Square
London
W1P 6BT

•••

39% of us eat sausages once a week. 29% only eat them once a month.

Chips are the big sausage platefellow in the 1990s, followed by eggs and bacon, and then by beans. But for late twentieth century under 24-year-olds, the sausage sandwich is the sausage mouthfiller par excellence.

•••